The "Ur-Nammu" Stela

Frontispiece. King bearing building tools, "good" face of stela, register III. UPM CBS 16676.14.

UNIVERSITY MUSEUM MONOGRAPH 110

The "Ur-Nammu" Stela

Jeanny Vorys Canby

University of Pennsylvania Museum
of Archaeology and Anthropology
Philadelphia

Library of Congress Cataloging-in-Publication Data

Canby, Jeanny Vorys.
  The Ur-nammu Stela / Jeanny Vorys Canby
      p. cm. - (University Museum monograph ; 110)
  Includes bibliographical references and index.
  ISBN 0-924171-87-1 (alk. paper)
  1. Ur-nammu Stela. 2. Iraq-Antiquities. I. Title II. Series.
  DS69.5.C34 2001
  935-dc21
                                          2001002418

Printed in the United States on acid-free paper.

For the "cheering section":

Yellott and Mac Canby
Adeline Werner Vorys

Publication of this volume was made possible in part by
a generous subsidy from the Hagop Kevorkian Fund.

Contents

List of Plates

Acknowledgments

Robert Dyson, former Director of the University of Pennsylvania Museum, must be credited with the impetus for this project, since he suggested the possibility of dismantling the Ur-Nammu stela on the same day in 1986 that he welcomed me to look through the fragments of the monument in storage.

That dismantling was done systematically by Tamsen Fuller, who matched her usual competent, easygoing expertise with endless ingenuity. Many different ways of moving each awkward piece, tightly stuck or doweled to other pieces, were devised. She dislodged plaster from relief with a sure, light tap of a geologist's pick. When I asked where she had learned how to do this, she admitted she had never tried it before. The dismantling and conservation of the stela was made possible by contributions from the Hagop Kevorkian Fund, the Carpenter Foundation, and various private donors.

Visitors often commiserated humorously about the battered scraps we were so serious about. Indeed, the publication of such poorly preserved material would not have been possible without the intelligent specialists who grasped the importance of documenting any trace of relief on this rare monument. The artist Kathleen Gallaghan conscientiously studied and drew many of the "leftovers" from the 1927 reconstruction. Veronica Socha, who carefully analyzed and drew the well-preserved areas of relief, was equally earnest about very worn fragments. Similarly, UPM photographer H. Fred Schoch took care to make every detail of a fragment of clothing or unknown object clear. Unless otherwise indicated, all photographs are mine or the UPM's.

Only an old friend would have undertaken the thankless task of reading the first draft of the manuscript. This was Ellen Kohler of the Gordion Project, who meticulously corrected and rearranged it to make sense. Helen Schenck also deserves special thanks for her later, mercifully unintrusive editing and her singular patience and sense of the importance of the difficult subject matter.

Richard Zettler, current curator of the collection, has been gracious and helpful throughout.

Thanks are also due to the helpful members of the Department of Western Asiatic Antiquities at the British Museum for, among other things, letting me comb through fragments there in search of a missing piece of the stela in 1986—and are due especially to Julian Reade, who found it in Egyptian storage in 1996.

Jes Canby
1997

Abbreviations

AfO	*Archiv für Orientforschung* Vol. 22. Vienna, 1968/69.
AJ III	C. Leonard Woolley, "Excavations at Ur of the Chaldees." *Antiquaries Journal* III, no. 4 (October 1923), pp. 311–333.
AJ V	C. Leonard Woolley, "The Excavations at Ur, 1924–1925." *Antiquaries Journal* V, nos. 1, 4 (January, October 1925), pp. 1–20, 347–400.
AJ VI	C. Leonard Woolley, "Excavations at Ur, 1925–6." *Antiquaries Journal* VI, no. 4 (October 1926), pp. 367–424.
Amiet, *L'art d'Agadé*	P. Amiet, *L'art d'Agadé au Musée du Louvre.* Paris: Éditions des Musées Nationale, 1976.
BK	J. Börker-Klähn, Altvorderasiatische Bildstelen und vergleichbare Felsreliefs. *Baghdader Forschungen* 4, 2 vols. Mainz am Rhein, 1982.
Canby 1987	J. Canby, "A Monumental Puzzle." *Expedition* 29, no. 1 (1987), pp. 54–64.
Canby 1993	J. Canby, "The Doorway on the Ur Nammu Stele." *Istanbuler Mitteilungen* 43 (1993), pp. 147–150.
Canby 1993a	J. Canby, *Sumer: Cities of Eden.* Alexandria, VA.: Lost Civilizations, Time-Life Books, 1993, p. 138.
Canby 1998	J. Canby, The Stele of Ur-Nammu Reconsidered. *XXXIVème Rencontre assyriologique internationale, July 6–10, 1987, Istanbul.* Ankara: Türk Tarih Kurumu, 1998.
Exp	*Expedition*, Magazine of the University of Pennsylvania Museum of Archaeology and Anthropology, Philadelphia.
Frankfort, *A and A*	H. Frankfort, *The Art and Architecture of the Ancient Orient*, 4th rev. ed. Baltimore, MD: Penguin, 1970.
Frankfort, *CS*	H. Frankfort, *Cylinder Seals.* Reprint, 1965. London: Gregg Press, 1939.
Jacobsen, *Harps*	T. Jacobsen, *The Harps that Once...* New Haven, CT: Yale University Press, 1987.
JNES	*Journal of Near Eastern Studies.* Chicago: Oriental Institute.
Metzger, *Königsthron*	M. Metzger, *Königsthron und Gottesthron.* Novkirchener: Kevelaer, 1985.
MJ 16	C. Leonard Woolley, "The Expedition to Ur." *The Museum Journal* 16 (1925), pp. 27–55.

MJ 18 | L. Legrain, "The Stela of the Flying Angels." *The Museum Journal* 18 (June 1927), pp. 75–98.

Moortgat, *Art* | A. Moortgat, *The Art of Ancient Mesopoamia*, trans. J. Filson. London: Phaidon, 1969.

PKG 14 | W. Orthmann et al., Der Alte Orient. *Propyläen Kunstgeschichte* 14 (1975).

Porada, *PM* | E. Porada, The Collection of the Pierpont Morgan Library. *Corpus of Ancient Near Eastern Seals in North American Collections*, Vol. I. Washington, DC, 1948.

RA XXX | L. Legrain, "Restauration de la stèle d'Ur-Nammu." *Revue d'assyriologie* XXX (1933), pp. 111–115.

Spycket | A. Spycket, La statuaire du Proche-orient ancien. *Handbuch der Orientalistik* VII, 1, 2b, 2. Leiden-Köln: E. J. Brill, 1988.

Susa Cat. | *The Royal City of Susa*. Ancient Near Eastern Treasures in the Louvre, Exhibition Catalogue, eds. P. Harper, J. Aruz, F. Tallon. New York: The Metropolitan Museum, 1992.

Tello | A. Parrot, *Tello: Vingt campagnes de fouilles 1877–1933*. Paris: A. Michel, 1948.

UE IV | C. Leonard Woolley, The Early Periods. *Ur Excavations* IV. London: Joint Expedition of the British Museum and the Museum of the University of Pennsylvania to Mesopotamia, 1955.

UE V | C. Leonard Woolley, The Ziggurat and Its Surroundings. *Ur Excavations* V. London: Joint Expedition of the British Museum and the Museum of the University of Pennsylvania to Mesopotamia, 1939.

UE VI | C. Leonard Woolley, The Buildings of the Third Dynasty. *Ur Excavations* VI. London: Joint Expedition of the British Museum and the Museum of the University of Pennsylvania to Mesopotamia, 1974. Written in 1935.

UE VII | C. Leonard Woolley and Max Mallowan, The Old Babylonian Period. *Ur Excavations* VII, ed. T. C. Mitchell. London: Joint Expedition of the British Museum and the Museum of the University of Pennsylvania to Mesopotamia, 1976. Written in 1969.

UE VIII | C. Leonard Woolley, The Kassite Period and the Period of the Assyrian Kings. *Ur Excavations* VIII. London: Joint Expedition of the British Museum and the Museum of the University of Pennsylvania to Mesopotamia, 1965.

UET I | C. J. Gadd and L. Legrain, Royal Inscriptions. *Ur Excavations*, Vol. I. *Texts*. London: Joint Expedition of the British Museum and the Museum of the University of Pennsylvania to Mesopotamia, 1928.

Ur 'of the Chaldees' | C. Leonard Woolley, *Ur 'of the Chaldees'*, rev. ed., ed. P. R. S. Moorey. Ithaca, NY: Cornell University Press, 1982.

Winter 1986 | I. Winter, "The King and the Cup." In *Insight through Images, Studies in Honor of Edith Porada*, ed. M. Kelly-Buccellati, P. Matthial, M. Van Loon. Malibu, CA: Undena Publications, 1986, pp. 253–268.

Winter 1987 | I. Winter, "Women in Public: The Disc of Enheduanna." In *La Femme dans le Proche-Orient Antique*, ed. J. M. Durand. *RAI* 33. Paris: Editions Recherche sur les Civilisations, 1987, pp. 189–201.

ZA | *Zeitschrift für Assyriologie und vorderasiatische Archäologie*. Leipzig: W. de Gruyter.

CHAPTER 1

Introduction

DISCOVERY

The stela published here[1] comes from Ur, an important ancient city in southern Mesopotamia. It has always been attributed to Ur-Nammu, king of that city ca. 2100 B.C., because his name was inscribed on a robe of one of the figures.[2] We now know that this inscribed fragment came from a different stela.[3] Nonetheless, a date for the monument sometime during the century when Mesopotamia was dominated by the Third Dynasty of Ur (founded by Ur-Nammu) is implied by both its subject matter and style.

Both faces of the ca. 3.20 m high limestone monument were decorated with five registers of relief, 1.52 m wide, portraying the ritual activities of a king and the events accompanying these.

The monument was found in pieces in 1925 by a joint expedition from the Museum of the University of Pennsylvania in Philadelphia and the British Museum in London, under the direction of C. Leonard Woolley (later Sir Leonard). At that time, Ur-Nammu was the earliest of the Mesopotamian kings thought to be historical figures, and his stela was considered the crowning glory of the expedition's first three seasons. Woolley, much to his credit, particularly in that era, painstakingly collected the poor scraps of the monument along with the large blocks and well-preserved small fragments, and these miniscule fragments have added details to the scenes. Woolley also pioneered in describing the find circumstances of objects in detail, attempting when possible to make history from them. Still, he could not be everywhere his men were digging, and he did not see everything that happened. In 1925 he employed between 200 and 250 workmen, had only one assistant and made his own architectural drawings.[4] As is discussed below, Woolley's accounts of his discoveries sometimes do not correspond with each other or with the plans of the city, and the latter may disagree with plans of smaller areas. The extensive preliminary reports are sometimes identical to sections in the final publications but on other occasions give a fuller and somewhat different account of the discovery of objects. It is essential therefore to consult not only the final publications but also the reports, both those in the British *Antiquaries Journal* and those in the University of Pennsylvania's *Museum Journal*, as they are not identical.

The first fragment of the stela, in the Ur excavation field register U.305 (here catalogue no. 18[5]), was found during the 1922–23 season "in the S.E. entry-court of the [Enunmakh] temple by the outer gateway."[6] Since Woolley attributed it to a governor of Ur in the time of Ashurbanipal, the king of Assyria in the seventh century B.C., we can assume it came from late

---

[1] The stela, reconstructed in 1927, left enough empty spaces to encourage further speculations about the original appearance of the monument. All of the restorations have misled those who understood them to be accurate. This includes my own attempts in 1987 and 1993, which were premature and which I now sincerely regret. The current project alerted me to the pitfalls of speculating about an inadequately illustrated monument, one that had been hastily described, reconstructed, and published. Plaster on the stela hid not only damage but the edges of fragments, the joins or spaces between them, even parts of relief. A real look at the reliefs, the carving, the kind of stone, and its condition was possible only after dismantling and cleaning the pieces. In addition, the scenes took on clearer meaning as new details emerged on some of the hundreds of additional fragments which had been stored at the Museum.

[2] The name is now read alternatively, "Ur-Namma"; see Appendix 1 and M. Civil, "On Some Texts Mentioning Ur-Namma," *Orientalia* n.s. 54 (1985), p. 27, n. 1 (Rome: Pontificum Institutum Biblicum).

[3] Cleaning has revealed that the fragment with Ur-Nammu's name on it, **D1**, Appendix 3, is not the same stone as the stela. However, William Hallo, a Sumerologist at Yale University who specializes in the period, argued in the 1995 American Oriental Society meetings in Philadelphia that other evidence, particularly the inscription that names the canals dug by the king, proves the stela was made for Ur-Nammu. For a different conclusion, see Steve Tinney, Appendix 1. The city is thought by some to be "Ur of the Chaldees," whence Abraham set forth (Genesis 11.29–31).

[4] *AJ* V, pp. 347–348.

[5] See note 1, Chapter 4, for discussion of accession and catalogue numbers of the stela fragments.

[6] *AJ* III, p. 324 and pl. XXXIII; it is not clear which of the two gates on the plan is meant: in the catalogue in *UE* VI, p. 88 the findspot is given as "NW guard chamber of the gateway from the Dublal-mah courtyard to the Sacred Way" while in ibid., p. 54, when discussing the Enunmakh, it is described as "in the north corner of the central court."

debris. A few other pieces were found in the same season.[7]

Most of the stela fragments were uncovered in February 1925, almost by chance, as Woolley tells it. In 1924, the British Museum had been unable to provide its half of the cost of the coming expedition but the season took place anyway, thanks to donations from friends in London. When these funds ran out in January 1925, British residents in Iraq supplied the British Museum's half of the cost of the work, which allowed Woolley to dig for another month.[8] He wrote that this let him

> clear the west corner of the [Dublalmakh] courtyard and further ranges of rooms flanking E-dublal-makh. ... Had this work not been done in the present season it might well never have been done at all, for it is never very tempting to polish off the odd corners left over from a previous year, especially when there is no reason to suppose that anything of value will be found; even as it was I hesitated to spend money on continuing what had been hitherto the unremunerative task of digging down through seven feet of hard soil to a brick pavement, and it was more obstinacy than anything else that made me go on.[9]

The "unremunerative task" had been performed earlier in the season when Woolley dug down elsewhere to this same courtyard and found the "wreck of statues smashed to atoms by some enemy." He had been discouraged, and had written:

> [I]t is tantalizing to recover on such the inscriptions which tell that these were the offering or even the portrait figures of early kings of the city; but the destroyers have done their work only too well, and bits of the same sculpture may be found hundreds of yards apart, and though all are sedulously collected there is small chance of reconstructing anything entire.[10]

Later, however, in the west corner of the same court, dug in February 1925,

> [a]lmost the first day produced in one room a door socket of king Bur-Sin (2200 B.C.) with an inscription in 52 lines giving the history of the temple's beginnings, a very welcome record;[11] but it was in the western wing of the great court that the discovery was made which overshadowed all others. Here the pavement was littered with blocks and lumps and chips of limestone ranging in size from four feet to an inch or less, some rough, others carved, some pitted and flaked with the action of salt, some as smooth and sharp as when the sculptor finished his work; and all, or nearly all, belonged to one monument, the most important yet found at Ur.[12]

Woolley described the location of the fragments with care (Pl. 4b):

> The great monument has been broken up in antiquity, and its pieces were found by us strangely scattered—two near the east corner of the E-Nun-Mah, two utilized as the bases for impost-boxes in the building north-west of the Ziggurat, some in Room 17 of the E-Dublal-Mah, more on the pavement of the courtyard round the well, and the bulk to the south-west of the E-Dublal-Mah shrine, between it and the door of Room 33 or just inside that door. ... The proximity of the bulk of the pieces, and the heaviest, to the brick base of Ur-Engur [Ur-Nammu] incorporated in the court pavement by the south corner of the sanctuary platform makes it tempting to assume that the base was that of the stela ... but about this there can be no certainty.[13]

The base measured ca. 5.00×3.00 m. It was in part hidden beneath the courtyard.[14] Woolley specifies that it was made of brick of the Ur-Nammu period set in bitumen. He mentioned no stamps on the bricks and was presumably dating them by their size.[15] In the final publication written ten years later, contradicting

---

[7] Woolley referred to these pieces in a letter (now in the archives of the University Museum) dated March 3, 1925, to the Museum director. There he notes that most pieces of the building scene were found in 1923 and that they were (at the time of writing, 1925) in Philadelphia. I assume this comprises all the fragments he recognized from that scene, catalogue nos. **15–25**; however, **18**, **22**, **23**, **25**, and **27** were among the objects from Ur shipped to Philadelphia on the S.S. "London Marine" on November 17, 1925 (the original shipping list is in the archives of the Western Asiatic department of the British Museum).

[8] *AJ* V, p. 347.

[9] *MJ* 16, p. 50.

[10] For debris, see the report of January 31, 1925 in *MJ* 16, p. 43;

for the inscription on the statue and weight of Šu-Sin found here (now in Baghdad) see *UET* I, nos. 73, 74.

[11] For Bur-Sin (now read Amar-Sin) socket, *UET* I, no. 71, p. 16.

[12] *MJ* 16, p. 50.

[13] *AJ* V, pp. 399–400. Room 17 was probably the findspot of **14c**.

[14] The base incorporated (*UE* VIII, p. 19) in the Kassite period was "flush with and encorporated in the pavement of the court and was partly hidden by podium of the shrine" (*UE* VI, p. 107, n. 105).

[15] Woolley gives the size of the bricks: 0.30 m square × 0.05–0.06 m thick (*UE* VIII, p. 19).

his earlier report, Woolley claimed that there was nothing to connect the stela and the base, saying that only a few fragments of the former lay close to the base.

The earlier report rings truer. Two of the fragments from the pavement are certainly too big to have been moved very often: catalogue nos. **28a** (the left side of the third and fourth registers of the "poor"[16] face), weighing approximately 298 kg, and **12** (two thirds of the second register, both faces), weighing approximately 218 kg.[17] Moreover, the large pieces that joined these two—**28b–28d** (the inscribed band and fifth register on the poor face) as well as **14d–14f** (the right side of the second register of the good face)—lay in the same pile. Also found there were two large fragments (**1** and **6**) of the top registers. Other large sections of the stela, such as the building scene on the good face, are represented by surface chips left behind on the court when the large fragment beneath them was taken elsewhere. It seems unlikely that anyone would drag so much of the original stela here in pieces from where it was broken up. It would seem more probable that the stela stood on the Ur-Nammu–period base and was destroyed in situ.

Several fragments had been reused. The two fragments reused as door-post sockets in impost-boxes (**14a**, **14b**; Pl. 8c, d)[18] were in chambers of the Kassite period (fifteenth century B.C.) on the ziggurat terrace. These joined four (**14c–14f**) lying with the large group on the court.[19] The last of the pieces of the stela, the wrestlers (**29**), found in 1932, also came from the ziggurat terrace. It had been used as sub-flooring under

the northeast edge of the court of the Kassite Ningal temple.[20] Again, it joined a small upper left corner fragment from the pile on the court that was stored in the University Museum.

From the beginning, the two museums agreed that the pieces of the stela should be kept together.[21] As a result, in the division of finds in 1925, the stela was deemed equal to all the other objects from that season.[22] A drawing of lots gave it to Philadelphia. The pieces were exhibited in London before being shipped to Philadelphia in November 1925.[23] The frequently illustrated reconstruction of the second register with parts of the registers above and below (catalogue nos. **12** good face and **14a–f**) was made at this time (Pl. 3b).[24] The right corner of the top register was restored with the skirt bearing Ur-Nammu's name, **D1**, Appendix 3, in front of the seated god there. The face of the god, which had been lost, and the heads of the kings in register II were reconstructed in plaster. The less well known panel containing the first reconstruction of the butchering and standards scene (**12** poor face) was probably also made at this time.[25]

By 1927, the five large fragments and twenty-three smaller ones had been made into a stela in situ in a gallery in the University of Pennsylvania Museum (Pls. 1, 2).[26] The heads of the kings and the right arm of the right king, register II, good face, were reconstructed differently than in the previous London restoration. The heads of the minor goddesses in the same register were restored.

The reconstruction was supervised by Leon Legrain, curator of the Babylonian Section, a Sumerol-

[16] See Chapter 4, p. 29. As explained there, the two faces of the stela are designated "good" and "poor," terms which reflect the general condition of the surface on each side and replace the terms "obverse" and "reverse" used in *UE* VI, for which there is no evidence.

[17] Woolley did not mention the fact that the lower left fragment of **12** good face, with the scene of the throne and dias, had been reused as a door-post socket (Pl. 7d). It is difficult to tell from the condition whether the piece with the socket was used when it still lay beside the main block of **12** with the king and goddesses, or was used elsewhere.

[18] An "impost" is the element at the top of a door frame where the pole on which the door was hung fitted. I assume that by "boxes" Woolley means that the sides of the fragment with the socket were surrounded by a frame of bricks.

[19] See Chapter 4, catalogue entry for **14** and n. 19 for discrepancies between reported findspots of the fragments from impost-boxes.

[20] *UE* V, p. 55; *UE* VI, p. 103.

[21] Unlike the fragments of the Gudea stela (see below), where one part of a fragment ended up in Istanbul and another of the same in Paris, see *BK* nos. 46, 61b, 63b, 78b, etc.

[22] Letter, C. H. Harrison to Sir Frederic Kenyon in London, April 14, 1927 (BM Western Asiatic Archives).

[23] Aboard the S.S. "London Marine" (see n. 7 above). The original shipping list has rough sketches of the pieces, which it lists individually with measurements. These have proved very useful in piecing together the post-excavation history of the monument, including such information as the dates of different reconstructions and the trimming done for the 1927 restoration in Philadelphia.

[24] A sketch of the right side of the 1925 reconstruction is in the shipping list, see previous note. The photograph of this reconstruction continued to be published long after the subsequent 1927 reconstruction was completed, see *UE* VI (1974), pl. 43a; R. Dyson, "Archival Glimpses of the Ur Expedition in the Years 1920 to 1926," *Exp* 20 (1977), pp. 16, 19; S. Lloyd, *The Archaeology of Mesopotamia*, rev. ed. (New York: Thames and Hudson, 1984), p. 156, fig. 107; *Susa Cat.*, fig. 47.

[25] *UE* VI, pl. 44a. It is shown, incorrectly reconstructed, on the 1925 shipping list without catalogue no. **46**, added to the scene later.

[26] *UE* VI, pl. 41a, b. The date is established by a letter, E. J. Gadd to L. Legrain, April 27, 1927, thanking him for a photograph of the restored stela (UPM Archives, "Administrative Records. Near East Section, Legrain Correspondence, 1924–28").

ogist and one of the epigraphers of the Ur expedition. Paul Casci, who had been lured from Florence where he was working with his father reconstructing objects in the Uffizi Palace, was the restorer.[27] In June 1927 Legrain published a lengthy description of the scenes on "The Stela of the Flying Angels," as he dubbed it, in the University's *Museum Journal*.[28] There a photograph showed the lower three registers of one face on catalogue no. **28** already reconstructed in the gallery. A rod steadied the reconstruction and the wooden frame behind it was bolted into the floor (Pl. 9d).[29] In 1933, Legrain published photographs of the completely reconstructed monument with a brief description in *Revue d'assyriologie*.[30]

Woolley's own description, written by 1935, finally appeared in 1974 in the sixth volume of the site publications, *The Buildings of the Third Dynasty*.[31] This included the important fragment showing a wrestling scene (**29**), found after Legrain's 1927 article was published. The only additions made in 1974 to Woolley's 1935 manuscript were two plates illustrating 17 other stela fragments then in storage at the Museum.[32]

The scene in the second register, good face, showing the king before a seated deity, is a very common one, and the monumental version of it on the stela became virtually the classic example of Mesopotamian art. It and the entire good face of the stela have been illustrated in many publications. However, it was difficult actually to see the reliefs because of the size of the monument. The fifth register lay between 0.20 and 0.64 m above the floor of the Museum gallery. The famous second register was 1.50 m higher. It was necessary to lie on the floor to see the former or stand on something to see the latter. This may explain why no one ever noticed that the original face of the god in the second register on **14** had been replaced by a cast (Pls. 3a, b, 32). The "angels" floating at the top of the monument three meters from the floor could be seen only from afar. One face of the monument, here referred to as the "poor" face, is so worn that scenes are very difficult to discern. Because it was placed seven feet from the gallery wall, photography was very difficult. Only one very poor picture of this entire face was ever published (Pl. 2).[33] The unusual scenes there are consequently poorly known.

NEW RESEARCH

Only the lower half of the august deity seated in the top register of the good face survives. The figure is a common subject, but the toes of someone seated familiarly on his lap are unusual. They caused much speculation about the identity of both child and parent. In 1986 I was investigating the symbolism behind the ancient images of a child,[34] and, in hopes of finding more of the figure above the toes, asked Robert Dyson, then Director of the University of Pennsylvania Museum, if I might look for it among the pieces of the stela in storage. On catalogue no. **3** I found the hand that went with the toes, which proved that both ex-

tremities, unexpectedly, belonged to an adult. Moreover, in addition to the 17 fragments published in 1974, I found more than 50 that had remains of identifiable subjects in relief, plus dozens more with traces of scenes which are still mysterious to me. By good luck, the stela then stood in a gallery closed to the public. This allowed me to examine it close up from a ladder while using floodlights. It was possible to see where some of the new fragments joined the stela and that there were incorrect or seriously misleading restorations. The film of painted plaster covering these restorations sometimes spread onto the ancient relief

---

[27] The one serious miscalculation made in the restoration was placing **14** (good face) 0.06 m too low. The restorer forgot to add the width of the divider omitted from the building scene to the height of the building. Since the top of the building scene was in the bottom register of **14**, which also included parts of registers I and II, the whole good face was affected. To adjust for the mistake, the divider restored in plaster at the top of register III, poor face, was put artificially low and the figures in front of the building on the good face shortened. See also Chapter 2, nn. 6, 15, 23.

Unfortunately, the join that may still have existed between the back of the drummers (**28a**) and the back of the basket carrier (**25**) was lost when the latter was chiseled off to fit it in the wrong place behind the former (Pl. 9c)!

[28] *MJ* 18, pp. 75–98.

[29] *MJ* 18, p. 88, pl. Ve.

[30] "Restauration de la stèle d'Ur-Nammu," *Revue d'assyriologie* XXX (1933), pp. 111–115.

[31] *UE* VI, pp. 75–81.

[32] *UE* VI, pls. 43A, B. See Chapter 4, p. 29, n. 1.

[33] *UE* VI, pl. 41B; *RA* XXX, pl. II.

[34] J. Canby, "The Child in Hittite Art," in *Ancient Anatolia, Aspects of Change and Cultural Development: Essays in Honor of Machteld J. Mellink*, eds. J. Canby, E. Porada, B. Ridgway, T. Stech (Madison, WI: University of Wisconsin Press, 1986), pp. 54–69.

surface. All of this led me, in 1987, to propose a new, unfortunately erroneous, restoration.[35] Finally the Museum made the decision to dismantle the stela, remove the restorations, and clean the pieces, a process which was begun in October 1989.

The dismantling took only one month. It was done by conservator Tamsen Fuller, assisted only by a tall metal tripod and a winch—a remarkable feat since the fragments weighed up to 298 kg. Fortunately, the fragments had been waxed before being set in plaster so they parted easily with a few taps of the chisel or pick.

The cleaning and conservation, however, took months. The original soft limestone block had been quarried with the horizontal strata of the stone parallel to the surface on which the relief was to be carved. Due to weathering, the stone had in some areas deteriorated along the bedding planes close to the surface, causing the relief to lift and detach. In some cases, such as in the butchering scene (12 poor face), the pieces with the relief still lay upon the core of the stone (Pl. 7c). In others, for example the "angel" on 1 poor face, almost 0.03 m of stone under the piece that bore the relief had weathered away (Pl. 7a).

Woolley had consolidated these areas in the field by bedding loose fragments in plaster and reattaching them using shellac as glue. Much of this work was done before photographs were taken (Pls. 18, 20, 29) and since Woolley never mentioned it, the poor condition of the monument was unexpected (Pl. 7b). The shellac had deteriorated, so all the numerous chips that made up some fragments had to be disengaged and reattached with inert material. Metal rods that had held the monument together were replaced with plastic dowels. (See Appendix 2 on the conservation of the stela.)

The tonal drawings, penciled drawings in which shading was employed to bring out the condition and quality of the relief, also required much more time than expected, in part because I kept finding joining pieces, in part because repeated scrutiny and much speculation allowed me to discern traces of the lost relief. Slowly, a tell-tale edge on a formless mass would yield its suggestion of a recognizable shape. On catalogue no. 30, where virtually nothing of the original relief surface is preserved, I recognized the depression

between an arm and the thigh it is pressed against only after I realized that there was a wrestling scene on 29. Fortunately Veronica Socha, who made both the shaded and line drawings over a period of several years, thoroughly understood the project and sympathized with the problems it presented. She was as intent as I on finding any trace of ancient relief and portraying it exactly. This made her patient with endless revisions and able to find more than one important join. As a result, approximately seventy percent of the stela could be reconstructed on paper. The figures that still "float" loose, their position unknown, could almost fill the empty space (see reconstruction of these "floaters," Pl. 12).

Full and varied illustration seemed the best means of recording the battered monument. In order to make the material available soon, discussion of the iconography is limited to those places where it is essential to the understanding of the scenes. The line drawings are meant as simplified guides to what can actually be seen. The reconstructions are intended to show how the fragments went together plus what can be restored with confidence (Chapter 2). I found it useful to present the completed puzzle (the scenes detailed in Chapter 3) before describing its parts but the reader can easily reverse that order by beginning with the catalogue of fragments (Chapters 4 and 5) and then proceeding to the description of scenes (Chapter 3). The inscription was collated by Steve Tinney of the Babylonian Section of the University of Pennsylvania Museum (Appendix 1).

There is still room for study of the fragments in the University Museum that have not been catalogued here. More pieces of the stela may turn up in the future. It was only in 1996 that the long missing fragment U.6587 (our 66b), for years registered as in the University Museum, was found in Egyptian storage at the British Museum! As an incentive for further study, I include reconstructions that offer little more than the relative sizes of the "floating" figures from the lower registers (Pl. 12). I feel sure someone eventually can identify and "attach" them, as well as many of the now mysterious subjects of which clear details remain, e.g., catalogue nos. 56, 68, 69, and 71, to the stela.

[35] "A Monumental Puzzle," *Exp* 29, no. 1 (1987), pp. 59, 60, fig. 8. Part of this restoration proved seriously in error once the fragments on the stela could be closely examined. The "angel" block was put over the wrong face, see below Chapter 2, n. 8. Furthermore, the other angel was composed of catalogue nos. A1, from a different stela (see Appendix 3), and 75, a piece that still puzzles me.

ANCIENT SITE OF THE STELA

Something of the ancient history of the monument can be gleaned from the present condition of the individual fragments and the find circumstances. In spite of the discrepancies in the reports, it is possible to form an idea of the fate of what must have been a famous and familiar monument in the ancient city. It is of historical interest to learn how long it stood as an honored monument. Woolley believed that the stela had been broken up during the Elamite sack of Ur ca. 2000 B.C. The Kassites, who followed the Elamites, are known to have undertaken much building and reconstruction at Ur under their king Kurigalzu I (?–1375 B.C.).[36] Woolley thought that, just as the Kassites ca. 1400 B.C. had reused three pieces from the stela in buildings on the ziggurat terrace, they had used other fragments "in the Dublal-Mah buildings, and particularly in the building of the gateway (Room 33); when this was destroyed the stone fragments were flung down into the court and again wantonly smashed."[37]

There is no question that the stela was in pieces by Kassite times but Woolley's idea that the fragments had been broken a second time at the end of that period seems unlikely. He rather hesitantly proposed the theory to explain why what he called "freshly broken bits" were found lying on a "Kassite pavement." There are several problems with his theory. In the first place, the breaks on the fragments are not fresh. The few that look so are crisp not because destruction debris from the end of the Kassite period protected them until 1925, but because the section of stone on which they were carved was strong enough to withstand the ravages of time. Proof that some breaks that look fresh happened before the Kassite period is provided by those already broken fragments which the Kassites reused as door sockets (catalogue nos. **14a** and **14b**, Pl. 8c, d). The old breaks even now make tight joins to fragments (**14c–14f**) from which they have been separated for three and a half millennia. In contrast, the weaker stone of the left side of the same scene (in-

cluding the lower left corner of **12** good face, which was also reused as a door socket, see Pl. 7d) is partially worn and pocked. Drips of bitumen, a natural adhesive used as mortar in Ur, had leaked, probably remelted by some fire, onto the "freshly broken" fragments. There were also salt deposits on breaks. Both types of deposits show that the crisply joining fragments (**14a–f**) had suffered the same vicissitudes of exposure as the poorly preserved pieces of stone that lay nearby.

Woolley evidently assumed that the Kassites would not have left the broken monument on the court, but they probably did. The pavement on which the pieces fell (and on which they were found by Woolley) was not a Kassite pavement but one in use in Kassite times. It dated back to the Third Dynasty of Ur or to the following "Larsa" period.[38] We know that the Kassites found the fragments they used already lying on that pavement, because they left behind small joining fragments (mentioned above, p. 3). Other signs that the fragments had been picked over and moved around long after they were originally broken are drops of bitumen occurring on both the top and bottom breaks of a piece (Pl. 9a), and different degrees of wear on joining fragments. The pile may have become a sort of depository and quarry for reusable stone.

This supposition would explain some of the extraneous material Woolley found among the stela fragments, such as the broken Early Dynastic statue of Dada-ilum (U.2732, BM 119063). Bits of seven other stelae were also found.[39] Julian Reade has discovered that the fragments of the stela of king Utuhegal, now in the British Museum, actually come from two different stelae.[40] Among the relief fragments in storage in Philadelphia were parts of three other stelae (**A1–C2**), each of which is carved out of a stone different from that of our monument. Pieces of yet two more stelae were retrieved from the 1927 restoration: one is the fragment of a gown bearing Ur-Nammu's name, **D1**; the other a solitary fragment finely carved from dense

[36] T. Claydon, "Kurigalzu I and the Restoration of Bablylonia," *Iraq* 58 (1996), pp. 118–119. The court we are concerned with was connected to the (E)dublalmakh, the name of the building now translated by A. R. George "(House) of Massive Pilasters," in "The Bricks of E-SAGIL," *Iraq* 57 (1995), p. 186. Note that the pilasters he speaks of belong to the Larsa and not the Kassite period, see *UE* VII, pl. 117.

[37] *AJ* V, p. 400; see also *UE* VI, p. 76.

[38] *AJ* V, p. 388; *UE* VIII, pp. 11, 19. What Woolley called the "Larsa" period covers what is now usually called the Isin-Larsa or

even the Old Babylonian period, e.g., M. van de Mieroop, *Society and Enterprise in Old Babylonian Ur*, Berliner Beiträge zum vorderen Orient 12 (1992).

[39] Other fragments included here that look different stylistically from the "Ur-Nammu" stela are **45**, **47**, and **53**, see catalogue entries, Chapter 5.

[40] Julian Reade, "The Utuhegal Stela from Ur," *Baghdader Mitteilungen* 27 (1996), pp. 229–234. For the Dada-ilum statue and Utuhegal stela see *AJ* V, pp. 397–398 and fig. 2; *UE* VIII, p. 20; *UE* IV, p. 47, pl. 41c; *UET* I, no. 11.

white stone preserving part of a god with rod and ring, **E1**.[41] Appendix 3 catalogues all these stray pieces.

These bits from other stelae are frustratingly minuscule. We have only three pieces from one—two raft-like constructions and an unidentified object (**B1–B3**); from another, the head of a god and a lyre (**A1** and **A2**). It may be that these lonely remnants of other stelae are some of the small, plain, or "relatively unimportant" bits found near the Kassite well-head in the courtyard.[42] These lay almost 17 m southeast of the façade of the Dublalmakh building,[43] far from the other pieces, which suggests that some of the bits of other stelae may belong with the shattered debris discovered on the court floor earlier in the 1924–25 season, as described above.

It is unfortunate that we do not know whether the pavement on which the pieces fell was laid during the Third Dynasty of Ur or in the following period when power in Mesopotamia was held by the kings of the city of Isin and then of Larsa. If the pavement was of the latter date (ca. 2000–1900 B.C.), the stela could not have been destroyed by the Elamites when they sacked Ur at the end of the Third Dynasty. It could have survived, thanks, perhaps, to the rapid takeover of the city and expulsion of the Elamites by Išbi-Irra, the first king of Isin. The later kings' well-attested desire to link themselves to the Third Dynasty of Ur might even have protected the monument until the sack of the city in 1739 B.C. by Samsuiluna, the seventh king of the First Dynasty of Babylon.[44] In the end, the stela probably was toppled over. There are no signs of heavy blows on the relief faces. The breaks and flaking are mainly along natural cleavage planes (Pl. 8a, b). These could

be so flat that I at first thought that the surface between **28a** and **28b** was a cut made by the 1927 restorer (see Pl. 9a).

As explained above, the original position of the stela was probably on the base made by Ur-Nammu, near where the bulk and the heaviest of the pieces were discovered, as Woolley originally wrote (Pl. 5). The sides of the base faced the cardinal points. It thus stood at a 45-degree angle to the alignment of the court and surrounding monumental building[45] and to the alignment used much earlier in the ziggurat area probably by the builders of the Early Dynastic period.[46] However, a different tradition, one that used an orientation like that of the stela base, is represented by fragments of two phases of a sloping wall of the fourth millennium—late Uruk period—near the ziggurat (Pl. 6b).[47] The earlier phase was built with red bricks that were square in section, a crushed limestone floor, and large decorative clay cones with circular depressions at their base. The builders of the second phase of the wall used flat ash and clay bricks and small clay cones. The cones associated with these remains suggest that both phases were part of a religious complex.[48] In Mesopotamia the sacredness of certain sites was tenaciously preserved, and the peculiar orientation of the stela may have been linked in some way to these earlier structures. Perhaps a very ancient tradition sanctified the spot on which the stela stood. Later people still knew about it and revered it.

In Ur III times a visitor standing at the exit from the ziggurat terrace[49] turned right to face the thick wall surrounding the Giparu. This housed the high priestess of the city god, Nanna, and the temple of his wife, Ningal. The visitor would have seen one face of

---

[41] God with rod and ring, from E.S.B. = "Dublalmakh, building south-east of the court," according to the list in the University Museum archives, probably from room 17, the only room in that complex that Woolley mentioned in his description of the stela findspots, see n. 50 below.

[42] *UE* VI, p. 75.

[43] For well-head location: see plan, *UE* VIII, pl. 48; drawing, *Ur 'of the Chaldees'*, p. 222.

[44] For Išbi-Irra and his successors' relationship to Ur, see Piotr Michalowski, *Lamentation over the Destruction of Sumer and Ur* (Winona Lake, 1989), pp. 6–8; and William Hallo, in W. Hallo and W. K. Simpson, *The Ancient Near East, A History* (New York, 1971), pp. 84–93, 100. For Old Babylonian scribes' preservation of Ur III traditions, see ibid., p. 165.

[45] A base in the great "Court of Nanna," northeast of the ziggurat, had the same orientation: *UE* V, p. 79, pl. 77. For Woolley's opinion on a different location of the stela and the possible connection to the position of the god and goddess in register II, good face, see *UE* VI, p. 77.

[46] *Ur 'of the Chaldees'*, plan p. 115; ibid., p. 46. However, Woolley does mention a stretch of Early Dynastic wall, of baked plano-convex bricks on stone foundation, near the north corner of the Giparu—i.e., near the base for the stela—that was oriented differently than the Giparu, *AJ* VI, p. 366. Note that the use of plano-convex bricks does not necessarily prove the early date of a wall. M. Gibson found them still in use in Ur III times at Nippur; see "Investigation of the Early Dynastic–Akkadian Transition," *Iraq* 57 (1995), p. 5.

[47] E. Porada, D. P. Hansen, S. Dunham, and S. H. Babcock, *Chronologies in Old World Archaeology*, 3rd ed., ed. R. Ehrich (Chicago and London, 1992), Vol. 1, p. 99 and Vol. 2, fig. 3.

[48] *UE* V, pp. 5–6, pls. 11b, 13b, 14b, 67 (plan); *Ur 'of the Chaldees'*, pp. 36–37 and photo on p. 38.

[49] This was a simple gate. The front room of the later Dublalmakh did not yet exist. It is mistakenly shown on the plan of the Ur III city, *UE* VI, pl. 53 = *Ur 'of the Chaldees'*, p. 141. See the plan and description of the entrance to the ziggurat terrace of the Ur III period in *UE* V, pp. 26–27 and pl. 68; see also the different account in *UE* VIII, p. 20.

the stela on his left as he walked to the northwest entrance to this building. To see the opposite face he needed to jog to the right on his return to the ziggurat area. Southwest of the stela some buildings 3 m from the buttressed outside wall of the Giparu (see the corrected plan here, Pl. 5)[50] formed a passage that led to the imposing entrance to the temple on the far southeast façade of the Giparu.

The area saw major changes under Išme-Dagan, the fourth king of the following Isin Dynasty. The entrance to the ziggurat area was moved to a new set of wide steps in the northeast face of the terrace wall. The back of the old entrance was walled in and a room was added in front, turning the old Dublalmakh into a "shrine," a place of judgment dedicated to the moon god Nanna. The open space between it and the Giparu was now closed off by a gate chamber, room 33, lying flush against the north corner of the wall around the latter.[51] The stela would have been directly in the path between the "shrine" and the southwest exit from the court, forcing a semicircular swing around it. Perhaps we can speculate that it was left in this awkward position to remind people of the link of later kings to the famous Third Dynasty.

ARTISTIC EVALUATION OF THE STELA

The Third Dynasty of Ur, founded by Ur-Nammu, ruled all of Mesopotamia and part of Syria for the last century of the third millennium B.C. This is a remarkably well known period, thanks to thousands of contemporary cuneiform documents and to well-preserved physical remains in the city of Ur itself.[52] These reveal the complex administrative and economic system that made the state function. Information about historical events and cultural and religious aspects of the period is gleaned from year dates on texts and from dedicatory inscriptions on stone. More is learned from literary texts copied as practice exercises in the scribal schools of the subsequent Old Babylonian period.

The art of the Third Dynasty of Ur is, however, poorly preserved. Our broken stela formed a major portion of the corpus. Now, however, we have learned that the fragments from stelae belonging to Gudea, ruler of the nearby city-state of Lagash, sixty-eight of them published, may be re-dated to this period.[53] These stela fragments were found by the French at modern Tello from 1887 on, together with spectacular statues of Gudea now in the Louvre, works of art of an earlier period, and texts that essentially led to the discovery of the Sumerians.[54] Important fragments of the Gudea stelae excavated illicitly, including an almost complete top register, entered the Berlin Museum in 1897 and were published in 1906.[55] Between 1910 and 1914 the French published the large number of relief fragments they had found in 1905 and taken to Paris.[56] A few of the over two hundred the French left in the Istanbul Museum were published in 1926.[57]

These Gudea fragments come from several different monuments but they represent only a fraction of the seven stelae Gudea claimed to have set up. For the most part they are small, and, with the exception of the register in Berlin, cannot be combined into coherent scenes or long superimposed registers.[58] In contrast, the Ur-Nammu stela survives in large enough sections to show the original sequence of scenes. It contains, in fact, the longest series of scenes known between the so-called Standard of Ur made in the mid-

---

[50] These rooms, omitted from the overall Ur III plan (*UE* VI, pl. 53), are in *AJ* V, pp. 391–392, plan p. 387; *UE* VIII, pp. 16–17. They are dated by bricks of Amar-Sin (the third ruler of the Third Dynasty) found in rooms 4, 13, 16, 18, and 19 there, compare Pls. 5 and 6a here. Temple business records dating to Ibi-Sin (the last king of the Third Dynasty) were found between Ur III and later floors in rooms 8 and 9 and Woolley refers to "rough stones" at the Ur III level of room 20.

[51] For the "Larsa" city plan: *UE* VII, pl. 117; for the description of the Kassite rebuilding of the Dublalmakh: *AJ* V, pp. 385–397; *Ur 'of the Chaldees'*, pp. 218–225, drawing p. 222.

[52] Mieroop, n. 38 above.

[53] P. Steinkeller, "The Date of Gudea and his Dynasty," *Journal of Cuneiform Studies* 40 (1988), pp. 49–53; Michalowski, *Lamentation*, n. 44 above, pp. 2–3 summarizes the evidence for correlating the date of Gudea and Ur-Nammu with events in Iran.

[54] E. de Sarzec, L. Heuzey, A. Amiaud, F. Thureau-Dangin, *Découvertes en Chaldée* (Paris, 1884–1912), pp. 211–222, pl. 22, 4–6, pl. 25, 5, pl. 8 bis, 4.

[55] E. Meyer, *Sumerier und Semiten* (Berlin, 1906), pp. 28, 50, 55, pls. VII and VIII, left and right.

[56] G. Cros, L. Heuzey, F. Thureau-Dangin, *Nouvelles fouilles de Tello par le Commandant Gaston Cros* (Paris, 1910–14), pp. 283–296, pls VIII–XI. The same material was published by L. Heuzey, "Une des sept stéles de Goudea," *Monument Piot* XVI (1909), pp. 5–24, pls. I–II.

[57] E. Unger, *Sumerische und akkadische Kunst* (Breslau, 1926), figs. 43, 44.

[58] The reconstructions in *BK*, Inserts A–F, are speculative.

third millennium[59] and the Neo-Assyrian reliefs of the ninth century B.C.[60] It is, at present, the only reasonably well preserved royal monument from Mesopotamia that falls in the 400 years between Naram-Sin of Akkad in the twenty-third century and Hammurabi of Babylon in the eighteenth century B.C.

The stela has sections of perfectly preserved relief where the original quality of the sculpture can be seen. It is very sophisticated. It is much more subtle and accurate in its representation of the human figure than are the Gudea stelae.[61] Other than from these stelae, the art of the Third Dynasty is known primarily from vast numbers of dull, repetitive seals and sealings and some clay figurines and plaques.

In 1935 Woolley wrote a chapter on the stela for his volume on the Third Dynasty. He had to rely on his own and Legrain's descriptions and the few old photographs that existed rather than taking a fresh look at the monument, which by then had been in Philadelphia for ten years. He had studied the fragments of the Gudea stelae, which were at that time considered to be much earlier than the Ur stela, and found numerous similarities. He wrote: "It is quite certain that in this [the top registers] as in other scenes there was a strict parallelism and that the subject was repeated on either side of the relief."[62] He ended his chapter: "Admirable as the Ur stela is, it strikes no new note, but is the last of a series wherein every detail, it would seem, had become stereotyped and every bit of symbolism had been consecrated by custom; for all its perfection of technique, it is emphatically a work of decadence."[63]

Woolley's judgment has influenced scholars up to the present day. Most, like him, have taken the stela as proof that under the Third Dynasty, Sumerian art was uninspired. Even Henri Frankfort described the composition as static.[64] It is important to emphasize how wrong Woolley was. Because the pieces were so poorly illustrated, we have been forced to depend on his and Legrain's sometimes careless descriptions and these have distorted our picture of Third Dynasty art. As the following pages will demonstrate, Woolley's idea that there was strict symmetry overall was based on his own erroneous reconstructions. For example. the four scenes on the top registers do not repeat each other. Not only do the kings differ in size, stand in different positions, and do different things, the "angels" above them are also not identical. They fly in at different angles. The one over the single king bathes her face in the water she dispenses. The "angel" over the libating king holds her face as far as possible above her liquid. We should presume that the different poses had significance. When the ancient sculptor intended to repeat a subject—as he did in the second register of the good face—he repeated every detail.

The scenes are not stereotyped but are for the most part unique. Strangely, although considered the embodiment of Mesopotamian iconography, they have never been analyzed in detail. Some, like the homage to the temple structure on the third register of the good face or the wrestling scene on the fourth register of the poor face, are totally new versions of subjects that, like the bovine butchering, go back to the beginning of Sumerian civilization.[65] Others that look familiar have striking variations from the usual compositions. The objects in the hand of the god in the second register, good face, are not, for example, the famous "Rod and Ring" but a coil of five dangling strands of rope tied around four times, and a very long tapered pole. This is not the thin circlet and short rod that the god Šamas holds out to King Hammurabi on his stela or that other gods extend toward other kings.[66]

A libation before a living king, fifth register, poor face, has no parallels. The implied divinity of the royal figure far exceeds that of a king receiving officials in "presentation" scenes.[67] The crescents over the kings' heads in the top registers remain unique.[68] The fact

[59] Frankfort, A and A, pls. 36, 37.

[60] Frankfort, A and A, pls. 84–88. Some date the so-called white obelisk, BK no. 132, PKG 14, pl. 206, to the earlier Ashurnasirpal in the eleventh century B.C., see J. Reade, "Assurnasirpal I and the White Obelisk," Iraq 37 (1975), pp. 129–150.

[61] A. Moortgat's remark, Art, p. 68, that the Ur-Nammu stela is "completely analogous in style" to the Gudea stelae illustrates how misleading the published photographs have been. There are also differences in style between the Gudea fragments themselves. None of the over 300 Gudea fragments that I have been able to examine in detail has carving as refined and subtle as that on the Ur-Nammu stela.

[62] UE VI, p. 76.

[63] UE VI, p. 81.

[64] Frankfort, A and A, p. 51, also calls the composition hieratic. For Woolley's statements other than in UE VI, see Ur 'of the Chaldees', p. 178. In The Development of Sumerian Art (New York, 1935), pp. 112–114, in which he included appraisal of some of the Gudea relief fragments, Woolley contrasted the Ur-Nammu reliefs with the spiritual quality evinced in the statues of Gudea.

[65] Homage to a temple, here, Pl. 16a; bull butchering, PKG 14, pl. 91; wrestling, ibid., pl. 81a, here, Pls. 14d, 15.

[66] Frankfort, A and A, pls. 65 and 121. The rope on our stela could rather be the rope to tie enemies by the nose-ring used by Ishtar at the rock relief of Anubanini (turn of the third millennium B.C.) at Sar-i Pul, PKG 14, p. 301 and fig. 183, or Esarhaddon at Sinjirli, ibid., pl. 232; BK fig. 219, cf. fig. 218.

[67] Winter 1986.

[68] With the rare exception of terracotta chair backs(?) from Nip-

that no parallels for these elements occur in the mass of glyptic material underscores how wrong was Woolley's claim that the iconography on the stela was stereotyped.

The new evidence, combined with a close look at the familiar scenes and especially the first real scrutiny of the poor face, shows that the stela belongs to the very ancient tradition in Mesopotamia in which a situation is described in clear, brief detail. Here, the various aspects of kingship are shown, in part metaphorically, in part literally. It is not always clear which way to read a scene—the wrestling match is an earthly event but it is attended by a deity. We also do not know whether the events happened on a specific occasion or were recurring.

The monument differs from the preceding Early Dynastic and Akkadian battle-stelae in its quiet, religious setting but it is a worthy successor to the Akkadian monuments that just predate it. The elegance of the relief, the consistently delicate carving will, I think, astonish those who have known the monument only from old photographs. We have the rare luxury in the third register of the good face of gazing at the almost perfectly preserved face of the king and god. They are pleasant faces, impressively calm and serious but not intimidating. The full, somewhat fleshy features are well proportioned and smoothly integrated. They show that the interest in anatomical detail that characterized much of the art of the Akkadian period, and the remarkable success in depicting it, did not end with that dynasty. Many details are correctly modeled, with special attention given to the arm and chest muscles, the structure of the feet and ears. We see the collar bone and flexor carpi as well as the deltoid and biceps. The greater pectoralis, like the goddess's breasts, are shown under the clothing. The feet show the Achilles tendon, ankle bone, plump heel, arch and splayed outside of the foot, and the contours peculiar to the large and small toe. Likewise, the convex curve of the upper thumb and plump muscle below the thumb in the palm of the hand and the fingernails are shown. The details are never over emphasized, nor do the intricacies of hair, beard, or jewelry overwhelm the surface they cover.

Sometimes the composition too continues the innovations of the Akkadian period. The scenes on the stela may be in registers but one of these—the building scene—is double and suggests something akin to the unique open space on the Naram-Sin stela. The traditional pictures of a man before his god where the figures seem as motionless as those in a tableau are found on the stela; but there are also active scenes where careful observation has made the action believable. Angels float effortlessly at the top of the stela. On the poor face we see a workman brace himself, foot against a supine bovine's neck, holding the heavy animal steady while a partner reaches down into the chest cavity. Beyond him another figure lifts a goatskin as high as he can so that the contents gush to the ground in a heavy stream. The angle of the back, the arms bent out holding the animal's legs apart, bent in under the neck of the goat, make the poses convincing. Farther down on the same face we watch a wrestler as he reaches over cautiously, head pressed tight against his opponent's, to encircle the latter's buttocks. The sculptor's struggle with the arms of the "angels" and other poses are noted in the following pages.[69] These are new poses and they are not stylized or exaggerated as in some in earlier periods.

The spirit behind the new and experimental features on the stela descends directly from the Akkadian period. It is this that suggests the monument was carved not long after it ended. Support for the date comes from parallels to unusual subjects on the Gudea stelae—the elaborate chariot, giant drums, men at work on a building. The stela in fact provides almost our last view of experimentation within the canon until it reappears centuries later in Middle Assyrian art. On the other hand, elements in the formal scenes of worship presage those of later times which do become, through endless repetition, classical Mesopotamian stereotypes.

---

pur where a scene of royal libation to a seated god, almost identical to that of register II, good face, has a sun-disc within a crescent above the god, tree, and worshiper, L. Legrain, "Terracottas from Nippur," *Publications of the Babylonian Section* IV (Philadelphia: University Museum, University of Pennsylvania, 1930), nos. 207, 208(?), pl. XXXIX, pg. 28 = E. Douglas van Buren, "Clay Figurines of Babylonia and Assyria," *Yale Oriental Series, Researches* XVI (New Haven, 1930), nos. 1264–1265, pp. 261–262, pls. LXV, LXVI. Also see idem, "The Rod and the Ring," *Archiv Orientalni* XVII (1949), nos. 3, 4, p. 438, pl. X, fig. 2; and M.-Th.

Barrelet, "Figurines et reliefs en terre cuite de la Mésopotamie antique," I, *Bibliotheque archéologique et historique* 85 (Paris, 1968), no. 508, p. 288, pl. xlviii, from Tello. These seem to me more like decorative elements at the top of chairs, see N. Cholidis, "Möbel in ton," *Altertumskunde des Vorderen Orients* I (Münster, 1992), nos. 10, 11, 26, pls. 9, 10, 13.

[69] "Angels," top registers, on **1**; servant behind king, register III, good face, on **14**; worshiper with both hands raised, register V, poor face, on **28b**.

CHAPTER 2
Reconstruction

Six large fragments comprise about one third of the stela. With some 25 smaller fragments of relief, these allow a reconstruction on paper of almost two thirds of the scenes on the original stela (Pls. 10, 11). From these fragments we learn the size and shape of the monument, that it had five registers, that it was carved on each face, and that the condition of the stone can differ markedly, face to face.

Fortunately there is little doubt about where the larger fragments were originally located on the stela, thanks to two large surviving sections for whose relationship to each other there is good evidence. One section is made up of once-joining fragments **12** and **14**; the other section, of once-joining fragments **28a–28d**.[1]

The first of these sections contains, on **14**, the right side-face of the stela and three marvelously preserved registers on what, because of the condition of the surface, can be called the "good" face.[2] It is the middle register of the three that adjoins the good face of **12**, which preserves the left side-face of the stela. This complete register gives us the width of the monument, 1.52 m. The upper register of **14** shows the skirt of a seated deity and the tips of the feet of someone on its lap. The deity is one third larger than identical figures in the register below, which proves that it was in the top register of the stela. We know this because the same larger scale is seen on another fragment, **1**, which preserves a small segment of the side face of the stela slanting inward to form the typically rounded shape at the top of such monuments. Since the uppermost of the three superimposed registers on **14** is part of the top of the stela, register I, the middle register of **14** must be register II. The lowest of the three registers on **14**, only the upper half of which is preserved, must be register III. The piece from the top register, **1**, is carved on both sides, signaling that the stela had two faces.

In register III, between a god and a servant, is a king who appears to be involved in some sort of building activity since he carries building tools over his shoulder (Pls. 31, 32).[3] The building tools tie him to numerous fragments (**15–27**) that show men at work constructing a brick building. They climb up in front of it to work on top of it. The king is undoubtedly part of this large scene, which occupies the space of two registers.[4] I return to the reconstruction of the whole building scene below. The relevant point here is that, since the king and his companions in register III are not shown in front of the brick building, they must be standing on top of it. The building below them would therefore have been in register IV of the good face. One of the fragments of the scene, **22**, shows that below the building there was a high plain band instead of the usual narrow register-divider. The high band provides the evidence to tie the two large sections of the stela together, as is explained below.

The second large section of the stela, **28a–28d**, contains three registers on the left side of the stela, including the left side-face. The stone on which the scenes were carved contrasts strikingly with the fine-grained, hard stone of the section of the good face just described. It is soft and, in many areas, dissolved, flaked, or still flaking. There are numerous small holes and craters (see Pls. 38, 39, 41). An identical surface is seen on the back of register II on **12**, whose good face is described above. It is reasonable to conclude that the large, poorly preserved section **28a–28d** must have been on the same badly preserved face of the stela. In the present study, this is called the "poor" face, again referring to the condition of the stone.[5] The variation in preservation suggests that the layers of sediments in

---

[1] The way in which catalogue numbers (which are appended to the UPM accession number for the entire stela) were assigned to the individual fragments is explained at the beginning of the catalogue in Chapter 4.

[2] Replacing the old term "obverse," for which there is no evidence.

[3] The basket dangling against the king's shoulder was used to carry earth for making bricks, the plowshare for digging that earth, and the adze for shaping wood.

[4] The link between the figures is iconographical: there is no physical join between the servant behind the king and the building scene, as has been assumed for years because of Legrain's claim in *RA* XXX, pp. 111, 114. The leg that Legrain spoke of is **47** here, and joins a piece from storage to form one of the figures of unknown position. The leg was mounted under the servant in the 1927 reconstruction.

[5] This is what Woolley called the "reverse."

the stone run vertically (see Pl. 8a). In any case, the condition of the surface proved an invaluable clue as to which face a fragment had once belonged.

We know that the three registers of the poorly preserved section **28a–28d** can only fit on the left somewhere below the second register. There is no room for the section on the stela above the third register. Its former position is suggested by the wide band between registers IV and V. The band, which is inscribed, is the same height as the plain high band beneath the building on the opposite face (on **22**). We know that the registers and dividers on both faces of registers I and II are the same height, and that registers on one face lie directly behind registers on the other. The wide band on the poor face should then lie directly behind the corresponding band on the good face—that is, below register IV. The register below the band on the poor face will then be register V of that face. This means that the second large section **28a–28d** formerly stood on the left of registers III–V of the poor face. The drummers in the middle register of **28a** were originally back to back with the basket carrier before the building on **25**. The newly found fragment of the stela, **66b**, is a right corner with a section of plain, high band above symbols. Joining **66a**, it can only fit at the right end of the inscribed panel. It cannot be placed on the good face because it is too thick to be fitted behind **28b**.[6]

Another large fragment, **29**, can be assigned a secure place in the stela as so far reconstructed. It cannot have been in register V on either face because it has the normal register-divider above it instead of the high band. The fragment is too tall to be fitted into the third register.[7] Only register IV on the poor face can accommodate it. Confirmation of this position is given by a faint line marking the edge of the inscription that would have continued below the scene.

This large fragment, **29**, shows wrestlers and attendants with towels. A small fragment, **30**—one that joins no other physically—with the surface completely eroded, preserves the crease between an arm and the thigh it is pressed against. This surely belongs to the entwined wrestlers on **29**. A large, very worn right corner fragment of the stela, **31**, still bears telltale traces of the unique, high dais in the same wrestling scene.

The top register of the good face proved more difficult to reconstruct. On each face of the large fragment of the top register, **1**, there is a figure of a king with a goddess flying above him dispensing a liquid. On one face, a king stands back-to-back with another king facing right, of whom there is only the outline of cap and shoulder preserved. In front of the well-preserved king is the tip of a tree over which he must have been pouring a libation (Pl. 11). On the other face of **1** the king stands alone (Pl. 10). The critical question is, which of these two scenes was above the good face, and which above the poor face? In this case, the condition of the stone did not indicate how to turn the fragment, as I had thought when I published two preliminary and erroneous reconstructions.[8] I discovered the real condition only when the piece was seen close up after cleaning. Both faces are in some areas well preserved, and in others flaked or deteriorated. Fortunately, evidence for positioning the block came from a fragment that had been placed just above register II on the left of the good face in the 1925 and 1927 reconstructions (Pls. 1, 3b). We discovered that the dais and register-divider above the seated goddess is on a piece that actually joins **12**.[9] This was of great importance to discover because on top of the dais a thin sliver of a throne is preserved. A deity must have sat on it. Therefore, in the top register on the good face there was an enthroned deity at either side of the scene. The two seated deities would have left too little room between them for the two kings and sacred tree on the one face

---

[6] If joining surfaces on the backs of these fragments existed when found, trimming of the back of **25** during the 1927 restoration has removed any trace of them. See n. 23 below and Chapter 1, n. 27.

[7] Woolley, following Legrain, suggested it belonged on register III poor face, *UE* VI, p. 79. They did not allow for the divider above the scene. I know of no photograph of the poor face showing the fragment inserted in the stela.

[8] See Chapter 1, n. 35. In "A Monumental Puzzle," *Exp* 29 (1987), pp. 59–60 and fig. 8, unfortunately reproduced in the long-delayed publication of a 1987 lecture, Canby 1998, p. 46, fig. 12; and repeated in *Sumer: The Cities of Eden* (Lost Civilizations), (New York: Time-Life Books, 1993), p. 139. Before we had dismantled the stela the surfaces, seen from afar, looked different. The well-preserved background and plaster fill suggested to me that the scene with two kings belonged on the "good" face (Woolley's "obverse"), where the surface of the three registers on **14** is in such excellent condition. The photograph of the piece

propped up on a basket at Ur is misleading (a cropped version is *UE* VI, pl. 42a; here Pl. 20 top). Here the wax in front of the angel is visible but the extent to which the piece had flaked is not, because Woolley had already reattached the loose fragments. He never mentioned these repairs nor where he found the detached fragments. The photograph in *MJ* 18, p. 76 was taken after the plaster restoration was done.

[9] The fragment of a platform was not put there in 1927 arbitrarily, as Woolley claimed (*UE* VI, p. 76: "… even the throne platform of the Philadelphia reconstruction being unsupported by material evidence …"), but because it joined the register below along a thin edge. The join must already have been made at the time of the London reconstruction, i.e., by 1925, as it appears in the photograph of the latter, ibid., pl. 43a (= *MJ* 18, p. 85; Pl. 3b here), and on the sketch in the shipping list. Unfortunately I did not discover that the join was real until after publishing the restoration mentioned in the previous note. That restoration was based on there not being a throne here in the top register.

of the large top register block, 1. Only the single king on the other face could fit into such a scene. The single king had therefore to be above the good face of the stela.

When I put the single king in the center of his face of the stela, the back-to-back kings on the other side of the block fell exactly in the center of their face. This must have been what the ancient artist planned. Woolley's "parallelism" between the four scenes in the two top registers, a parallelism that he believed was typical of the whole stela, does not exist. It could never have existed. Woolley had overlooked the fact that the placement of the single king in the 1927 restoration threw the double kings on the opposite face far off center.[10] Actually, parallelism occurs only once on the stela, in register II of the good face.

Important small fragments can also be attributed to the top register of the good face where one king

stands between two seated deities. A well-preserved crown and hairdo of a deity (2) and the shoulder of a deity embraced by a hand (3) are both from a figure facing left, on pieces that almost join. The hairdo is masculine. The large hand belongs to an adult and, like the toes, must belong to the person sitting on the lap of the deity at right on 14.[11] The new fragments remove any uncertainty about the personalities in the intimate scene. It is now clear that an *adult*, not a child, sits on the lap of a *god*, not a goddess. Two plaques from Tello, Gudea's city, help restore the scene (Pl. 13a). On these, the goddess on the lap leans against the god's breast, twining her arm around his neck.[12] An inscription on the Louvre plaque identifies her as the wife of the city's god. The Ur stela may represent the city god of Ur, Nanna, and his wife, Ningal. The scene is rare, but it was also shown on an Early Dynastic sealing (Pl. 13b).[13]

---

[10] See restoration *UE* VI, pl. 41a. The bump behind the king's shoulder was thought to be the shoulder of the other king, see below Chapter 3, p. 17. In the 1927 reconstruction, the badly eroded back of the king was mistaken for the real edge of his body, which resulted in his being much thinner than the other kings on the stela. He was also too tall because the fragment was placed too high.

[11] The toes of the figure are also full size.

[12] The inscribed plaque from Sarzec's excavations is in the Louvre, A.O. 58, *Tello,* fig 35, g; Canby 1987, p. 61, fig. 11; E. A. Braun-Holtzinger, *Mesopotamische Weihgaben der frühdynastischen bis altbabylonischen Zeit, Heidelberger Studien zum Alten Orient* 3 (1991), no. W 24, p. 314, pl. 20 left. The other plaque is in Museum of the Ancient Near East of the Archaeological Museums in Istanbul, no. 5552, unpublished.

[13] CBS 11158, L. Legrain, "Some Seals in the Babylonian Collection," *Museum Journal* (June, 1923), pp. 142–143; idem, *Culture of the Babylonians* (Philadelphia, 1925), pp. 194–195, pl. XII, pl. LI; idem, *Seal Cylinders, UE* X (1955), no. 91.

Since this extraordinary sealing has never been published adequately, a brief description of the scenes is included here. There are two registers and at least twenty neatly carved, clearly impressed, mostly well-preserved figures. The faces have large noses and large round eyes over which are arched eyebrows. The gods have long beards that start at the cheek and descend in two or three strands over the chest. The deities wear a flat thick beret with horns at either side. These, in some cases, seem to turn over on themselves.

At the left edge of the top register are (1) the concave leg and two rungs of an elegant table or throne. To the right, emerging from a smudged and pinched area, is (2) the lower part of a figure in a tufted gown, facing right with back foot on a sphinx(?) right (as viewed) on a lion protome. Facing him, seated on a narrow, high-backed chair, is (3) a figure in a plain gown with bare proper right arm across his chest, left, covered. His feet rest on a double row of triangular mountain peaks. Then comes (4) a god with a long tripartite beard, *en face,* seated on a tufted stool, feet facing right, arm crossed over the chest. There are tufts on the bottom of his skirt. He has (5) a goddess *en face* sitting on his lap. She is identified by the curls over her chest which are shorter than the beards. Her arms are crossed over her breast.

This area, which is blistered and dark, includes (6) another god seated on a tall stool with thin legs, also *en face*. His large proper right arm is extended, hand bent up. He has a staff over his left shoulder (not rays, as in the drawing in Legrain, Seals, op. cit., p. 142). Behind him, *en face,* is (7) a well-preserved figure of a bearded god in a tufted skirt seated on a high, narrow stool. With both hands he holds over his chest a narrow-necked vase from which a stream curls up on either side. The ridge over his proper left shoulder may be the remains of liquid. Next to him stands (8) a figure wearing a skirt with fringes on the bottom, held up by a thick belt. He faces the divine couple. His proper right arm, bent over his chest, holds an implement that curves up over his shoulder. He leads (9) a figure by the wrist who wears a tufted cloak and carries a curved weapon (scimitar) over his shoulder. Another figure (10) in a tufted cloak follows.

At left in the bottom register all that remains is (11) the face of a deity facing right, and (12) the upper part of a bearded god, facing right, wearing a thick belt. He has a mace over his proper right shoulder and his left hand holding a mace(?) is extended. Facing him is (13) another deity in a three-tiered, tufted skirt with a thick belt, who carries a mace over each shoulder. He wears a long pigtail down his back and has feathered feet. Next, facing right, is (14) the lower part of a bird-man who carries a mace over his proper right shoulder. His proper left hand is placed on the shoulder of (15) another bird-man facing him, who carries a double-headed mace over his proper right shoulder and another over his left. He wears a beret with two feathers protruding. Both figures have wings and tail feathers over their feathered legs that end in wide claws. Behind the second bird-man is (16) a bearded god facing the same way, in a plain, wrap-around skirt and thick belt. He carries a mace over his proper right shoulder and a scimitar over his left. Behind him is (17) a floating, frontal face with a four-strand, wavy beard. It has a beret over which six circles are entwined. Behind the head is (18) another god facing left. His beret has something protruding from the middle. He wears a tiered, tufted skirt with thick belt, and carries over his proper right shoulder a four-pronged fork-like implement ending in knobs, and over his left a scimitar. Behind him comes (19) what may represent a lion-headed eagle, head down over a mountain or the horns of a small recumbent deer. Only the large wing with strongly marked striations is certain. The last recognizable figure (20) is that of a bearded god facing left with a mace over his proper right shoulder and a scimitar over his left.

The hairstyle of the restored goddess is drawn to match that of the goddess at left in register II below, with a long tress pinned up in back and two single locks hanging loose over the shoulders.[14] A fragment with a right arm outstretched, a vertical stream of water falling behind it (4), probably belongs to the goddess on the god's lap. Assuming that the water is the nearer stream flowing from the flying goddess's vessel to the foot of the seated god on this face, the arm is the correct distance from the goddess's shoulder. The arm is slightly smaller than the king's in the top registers but is larger than any arm in the registers below. It is extended as if it held something in the hand, which would have been between the streams of water. A vase filled from above and overflowing below, a well-known subject in contemporary art, seems appropriate (Pl. 14a).[15] A fragment of skirt (5) from another figure flying in from the left can only belong on this good face. (There is already a flying goddess in this position on the opposite, poor, face.) She comes in at an upward angle but just where is not known. I cannot guess how she held her head because the other flying goddesses assume quite different poses.

The astral symbols are restored from traces on a large fragment, 6, and must be placed at the peak of the good face because they are too large for the traces of a crescent preserved on the poor face of 1 (see discussion below).[16] On 6, the tip of a crescent is at the edge of the convex top of the stela. Its outside curve is preserved for 0.21 m. A small section of the inner curve, ca. 0.11 m from the tip, shows the thickness of the crescent at that point. Within the area circumscribed by the crescent are traces of two points of a star, or "radiant sun-disc" as some would call it, with a wide, undulating ray between them.[17] The size of the star was calculated from the angles described by the juncture of the lines of the points. When projected

around the center, the angles come closest to those of a seven-pointed star.[18] They are, however, not quite identical. The piece is so thick that it can only fit above the broken upper edge of 1 on the good face. Another fragment of a star point (7) is the correct size to belong to this sun-disc and has therefore been added.

Other small pieces can be attributed to the scene on the top register of the opposite (poor) face. A fragment with part of the necklace and beard of a large-scale king with arm extended, 8, can only belong to a king facing right.[19] A fragment of the tufted robe of a large-scale deity seated facing left (10) is the evidence for the god seated to the right of him. Another floating goddess above is represented by a fragment of gown (11) which fits none of the other air-borne goddesses.

Along the top of the preserved relief on 1 poor face three small remnants of the bottom edge of a crescent appear: two to the left of the left king's head, another to the right. A thick piece[20] of the crescent lies directly in front of the goddess's vessel. When the sections of the curve are connected, the lowest point of the crescent falls directly above the left king's head. It is not centered between the kings as might be expected. On a monument so meticulously planned, miscalculation of this order seems inconceivable. The symbol must refer specifically to the king on the left. The king on the right must be someone else.

Finally, we return to the building scene in the third and fourth registers of the good face with its upper right corner on 14. The rest of the scene is reconstructed from eleven small fragments, mostly relatively thin flakes, which show segments of bricks. No fragment joins another, yet together they provide the evidence to reconstruct much of the two registers occupied by the unique scene. They prove there were ladders leaning against the building, a door in it, a second

---

[14] The goddess on the Gudea plaques wears her hair in loose locks over the shoulders, like the goddesses on the Gudea stelae, compare *BK* nos. 41b, 48.

[15] For examples on the Gudea stelae, *BK* nos. 39, 40 = *PKG* 14, fig. 108, b, c and his seal, ibid., p. 239, fig. 44f (here Pl. 14a), and the basin in Istanbul, E. Unger, *Der Wiederherstellung des Weihbeckens des Gudeas von Lagash* (Istanbul, 1933); idem, *Sumerische und Akkadische Kunst* (1926), p. 98, fig. 47; Edibe Uzunoglu et al., *Istanbul Eskisark Eserleri Müzesi* (Turkiye Turing ve Otomobil Kurumu Yayini, ca. 1974), fig. 33. For water flowing behind the arm that holds the vase, see Georges Contenau, *Musée du Louvre, Les antiquités orientales, Sumer, Babylon, Elam*, pls. 14, 15; Moortgat, *Art*, fig. 188; and from Ur, *UE* IV, pl. 35, and p. 51.

[16] The curve along the edge of this fragment was trimmed off to fit the 1927 restoration! The real curve of the top register does not follow the battered upper edge of the floating goddess block (1) as the 1927 restoration suggested (Pl. 1).

[17] For the fragment U.6587, which sounds like it came from the astral symbol, see in the catalogue *UE* VI, p. 98 (there listed as in the University Museum) that it contained the "Upper portion of a frieze shewing right tip of crescent, upper part of angel's headdress, and tip and flat end of star rays to the left. Reused later as a door socket." This long missing piece (catalogue no. **66b**), recently discovered in the British Museum among Egyptian antiquities (letters from Julian Reade 1995–96), see below, joins catalogue no. **66a** (Chapter 4, following entry for **28d**).

[18] The type is known from Mesopotamia, see U. Seidl, "Die Babylonischen Kudurru-Reliefs," *Baghdader Mitteilungen* 4 (1968), no. 97, pp. 55–56, pp. 101ff.

[19] We found the necklace and beard under the plaster of the 1927 reconstruction of the king facing right, register II, good face. It can be seen on *UE* VI, pl. 43a.

[20] Found in storage.

building in front of it, and at least ten people surrounding it.

Eight people are represented by only a solitary arm, leg, or toe, each part revealing which way the person faced and whether he was on top or in front of the building. Moreover, because the sculptor always differentiated right from left foot and made the foot leading in the direction of movement the farthest from the viewer,[21] we can calculate which foot is missing and where it would have been placed. The bare legs show that the skirts were above the knee. We have shown them raised by analogy to the butchers' skirts in register II on the poor face (12).[22]

Catalogue no. 22, already mentioned, with the building above a high plain band, shows a ladder leaning against the structure and two figures facing left in front of it. Of each person, only a foot remains, the following (left) foot of the first one and the leading (right) foot of the second. Since the leading foot of the first person is not directly in front of his other foot, we have put it on the rung of the ladder. The top end of the ladder is preserved on another fragment, 18. The right, following, foot of someone standing on top of the structure facing right is seen above the ladder. He, and with him the ladder, has to have been somewhere to the left of the figures of king, deity, and servant in the upper right corner of the scene. That puts the bottom of the ladder in the left two-thirds of the scene.

A more precise location for it is provided by the other objects leaning against the building. A second ladder leans to the right, on 17. Only one side remains and because there is no trace of the other side to the left, we know it is the left upright. The large toe of the right, near foot of a person facing right standing above it remains. A separate structure is seen at the far left of the scene, on 15. Its smooth, sloping façade is in front of the brick building. A pole, or perhaps yet another ladder, leans against it. The approximate position of all the sloping objects can be fixed by allowing room for both feet of the people above the ladders and then projecting the ladders to the ground in front of the building without crossing them. The ensuing arrangement shows how wide the building was. It extended from near the left side of the scene to the right side.

There, a fragment which preserves part of the side face of the stela (25) shows a basket carrier in front of the building. His height and seven courses of bricks above him show that the brick structure was as high as a normal register plus a divider.[23] Three more basket carriers in front of the building are attested by fragments depicting upraised arms. One of the three (23), has traces of a left arm upraised in front of the upraised right arm of another figure, which proves the carriers were in a row. There is room for only four carriers between the left-leaning ladder and the right edge of the scene. Therefore, one of the upraised arms has to be that of the person we have supposed to be climbing the ladder on 22.

Evidence for the entrance to the building occurs on a small fragment that has the right side of a typical double-recessed or rabbetted door jamb (21). The whole door would have been at least twice as wide. The only space big enough for it is between the ladders. The door is far too short for the people in the scene but that is often the case in Mesopotamian iconography (Pl. 16a).[24]

The king, god, and servant in the upper right corner of the scene stand on top of the building. There were three or four more people with them there. Two of these are the figures above the ladders already mentioned (on 17 and 18). They face the corner figures and their place has been fixed. A figure who kneels facing left on the top of the building (on 16) must be located somewhere between the two standing figures and the sloping wall at left. There is one more fragment of a person with a right, leading foot standing on the brick structure. He faces left. It is arbitrarily attributed to the servant behind the king as it was in the 1927 reconstruction. Since it obviously does not join him it could instead be the leg of a seventh person on top of the structure, one who turned toward something at the far left of the scene.

---

[21] That is, the right foot of someone facing left, the left foot of someone facing right.

[22] We know from an Akkadian stela BK no. 21b, c. and a Gudea fragment, ibid., nos. 62, 87, that hems raised in front were shown on figures who stood as well as on figures in action.

[23] The fact that the building takes up the height of the divider was overlooked by the 1927 restorers, who put the top two registers a divider's height too low on the stela. They corrected for this on the opposite face by reconstructing a divider that short-

ened register III (28a), UE VI, pl. 41b. Unfortunately the join that may still have existed between the back of the drummer on 28a and the basket carrier on 25 was lost (Pl. 9c) when chiseling off the latter to fit in the wrong place behind the former!

[24] See the doors on the Gudea stela, BK no. 77, and on an Akkadian seal, O. W. Muscarella, ed., Ladders to Heaven, p. 88, no. 44. See on cylinder seals of the Protoliterate period, PKG 14, pl. 126c; Early Dynastic period, ibid., pl. 133e, f; see also Canby 1993a, p. 139.

CHAPTER 3

The Scenes

"GOOD" FACE

REGISTER I

A king, bare right arm raised, hand before his face, stands facing two streams of liquid falling to his right (**1** good face).[1] These overflow a vessel held by a goddess with a single pair of horns on her crown floating to the right above him. Legrain dubbed this figure an "angel"; Thorkild Jacobsen called such figures "mythopoeic representations of rainclouds."[2] The liquid undulates from side to side and in and out from the surface of the relief as it falls. The "angel" supports the round-bottomed vessel in the palm of her right hand and grasps its neck under the wide rim with her left. She lowers her head until the liquid of the nearer stream bathes her chin. A wavy lock of hair falls forward over her shoulder. Her dress, pleated lengthwise, covers her breast and shoulder (Pl. 18).[3] The pleats undulate as they flow behind her. The awkward attempt to represent the torso in profile is unusual and it is hard to guess where the missing left breast might have been. The face is charming, with a heavy-lidded eye, plump cheek, and short, straight mouth above the chubby chin.

The king holds out his left hand, perhaps to offer some small thing. There is no room here for a deity to be leading him to the god, as is often depicted in similar scenes on seals. He wears a round cap with wide turned-up brim under which three fine wavy strands of hair are pulled back from the brow, two more appearing at the temple. His robe is gathered in soft folds over the crook of his left arm. A fringed edge of the robe falls back at an angle beneath his right elbow. The other edge, which would have fallen below the left arm, is chipped off. He wears a necklace with three beads below thin strands. The upper part of the beard is defaced and the lower part is covered by his right arm. It is slightly tapered and twisted into eight strands. Despite much damage, the brow, eyebrow, the front of the eye with heavy lid and tear duct, most of the nose, and the inner edge of his raised right hand are still visible. There is a worn protuberance ca. 6 cm behind the lower shoulder blade. This is what Woolley took to be a part of the figure of another king, facing the opposite way.[4]

Facing the king is a seated god dressed in a tiered robe of thick strands clustered into tufts (**3**; cf. **14**, register II below). He is seated on a throne placed on a long, two-stepped dias. Like the altars found in households at Ur,[5] the façade of the throne imitates a monumental entrance to a temple—in this case with five recesses. The facade is unusually elaborate with a semi-detached column inserted in a deep recess between the second and third door frames from the outside.[6] Swags over the two inner door frames resemble those on the throne in register II below. The god's long hair, gathered into a thick bun with ends tied up by four ribbons, is covered by hatched lozenges (**2**).[7] Care has been taken to render the ear correctly, showing the helix, tragus, and anti-tragus.

A figure seated on the god's lap, toes dangling along the side of the throne, encircles his shoulder with a left arm (**3**). A rare Early Dynastic seal shows a similar scene (Pl. 13b).[8] Parallels on two plaques of the Gudea period from Tello (Pl. 13a) suggest that this figure is a goddess—probably Ningal, wife of the tutelary deity of Ur.[9] A carefully modeled bare right arm (**4**) is probably hers. It is extended and bent up slightly from

---

[1] Throughout this chapter the description of each register and the arrangement of figures in the scene is based on the reconstruction proposed in Chapter 2.

[2] *UE* VI, pls. 41a, 42b; for Legrain's "flying angels," see *MJ* 18, p. 75; for T. Jacobsen's term, see *Harps*, p. 393, n. 24.

[3] She is described as bare-breasted by Legrain, in *MJ* 18, p. 77, repeated in *UE* VI, p. 76.

[4] *UE* VI, p. 76. The protuberance behind the head in the old photographs is an optical illusion.

[5] *UE* VII, pls. 43b–46a and pp. 29–30. A tiny version of a household altar shaped like a temple entrance was also found, see ibid., pl. 97 (U.6195).

[6] The extra nitches are similar in principle to those of the throne on a stela fragment from Susa which is of the same period, *BK* no. 100, *Susa Cat.*, no. 110, pp. 169–171.

[7] This fragment of the god's head (**2**) does not physically join the torso fragment (**3**).

[8] See above Chapter 2.

[9] See above Chapter 2 for Tello parallels.

the elbow as if holding something, probably another flowing vase adding to the liquid falling at the god's feet. (The motif of multiple watering vessels was used a number of times by contemporary artists [Pl. 14a].[10]) The feet, here as elsewhere on the stela, are shown in careful detail. The leading, right foot shows on the inside face a high arch, Achilles tendon, plump heel, and smallish ankle bone. The first toe with nail indicated, is thick, the second much smaller. On the following, left foot, the small toe is contracted and the bottom of the foot is made flat and slightly splayed. The ankle bone is more pronounced (see Pl. 31). As discussed above (p. 15), the foot farthest back from the plane of the viewer is always shown in advance of the near foot.

On the left side of the top register there is a throne on which another deity must have been seated. The double dais beneath the throne, whose length might have suggested the gender of the deity, is, unfortunately, only partially preserved.[11] Above that figure there is another "angel" flying in at an upward angle from the left, the nine wafting pleats of her gown widening toward the bottom (5).

Over the king's head, at the top of the stela, is a very large star or radiant sun-disc,[12] floating free within a crescent (6, 7). The star points are outlined on the interior by two incised lines. Between the points on 6 is a wavy rectangle of fine rays.[13] The star and crescent symbol is well known but its position here is extraordinary. Symbols do not occur above kings or gods in Mesopotamian art until Neo-Assyrian times.[14] They are normally placed between worshiper and god. Another symbol in this unusual position is on the opposite face.

REGISTER II

At the far left a goddess sits facing right on a temple-façade throne placed on a two-stepped dais that,

unlike those of the god to the right and the god on register I above, ends short of the edge of the stela (12 good face). Her left arm, lower part bare, has open hand outstretched towards the king facing her. Her right arm is entirely bare with fist clasped and held to her breast. She wears an ankle-length garment made of eight overlapping tiers of thick wavy strands clustered into tufts. It has a double rolled border at top but is without the extra flap of material the gods have over their arms. Her breast rises under the thick garment. Like the angel, she has a plump cheek, rounded chin, and short upper lip. The tip of her nose is damaged and a break at the edge of her cheek gives the false impression that she is smiling. Her hair, gathered into thick wavy strands, is drawn from her forehead behind her ears. It is loosely bent up and tied with a thin ribbon wound around four times. The ends of the hair dangle. Another wide wavy lock, cut off straight, falls down over her bare shoulder between her breasts. She wears the usual crown, with four horns on each side tapering over a sort of peaked beret, and a collar necklace made of four thick bands, the topmost one tight under her chin. The disc of the crown, like others on this face, is cut off by the dividing band.[15]

In front of the goddess a king faces left and extends his bared right arm to pour a liquid from a conical vessel with a flat base. (The pinched pouring lip of this type of vessel is preserved near the plant at right, on 14.[16]) The liquid falls into a biconical stand with a rolled edge at the top (and bottom, as seen on the plant to the right on 14) and rounded band at the narrow waist. Growing in the stand is a short plant with gently pointed tip. On either side of the trunk are branches with wide median ridges and stiff oval leaves. Bag-shaped clusters of fruit on undulating stems hang over either side of the stand (see Pls. 25, 26).[17]

The king wears a simple bracelet on the right wrist. His closed left hand is held at his waist with the

[10] See above Chapter 2, n. 15, on multiple waterings.

[11] Had it fallen short of the left edge of the stela we could speculate that it belonged to a goddess, as in register II directly below.

[12] I.e., a star with rays between the points: a well-known Mesopotamian symbol. The fact that it floats free of the crescent is unusual.

[13] The crescent (6) as reconstructed in 1927 can be seen at the top of *UE* VI, pl. 41a. This is not block U.6587, ibid., p. 98 that Woolley described as having had a fragment of an angel's head as well as bits of astral symbols. That block, which we had thought was lost, has finally turned up; see cat. no. 66b.

[14] The sun-discs on the Naram Sin stela of the preceding Akkadian period, *PKG* 14, pl. 104, are at the top of the mountain,

high above the king's head. See also Chapter 1, n. 68 for one exception.

[15] Because the sculptor forgot to leave space or was the disc an afterthought?

[16] A bronze vessel of the same type is in The Metropolitan Museum of Art in New York, acc. 1994.45. It is inscribed, and identified there as Akkadian or Ur III (North Mesopotamia, Ur III, *Metropolitan Museum of Art Bulletin* [Fall 1994], pg. 8).

[17] Pers. comm., Naomi Miller, April 1999: "On morphological grounds, the 'bag-shaped clusters of fruit' are likely to represent fruiting date branches. Dates grow along a multitude of thin stems in the female date inflorescence. This can be seen together with a representation of dates from Puabi's tomb at Ur in N. F. Miller, 'Date Sex in Mesopotamia!' *Exp* 41, no. 1 (1999), pp. 29–30. I have no opinion about the 'short plant'."

bent left elbow protruding to the side. The left wrist area is broken. The lower part of his beard is twisted into seven locks, each ending in a curl. The body of the king is well preserved. The muscles of the arms, shoulders, and chest under the ankle-length robe are carefully rendered.

The bulge of the buttocks and the falling skirt reveal the lower part of the body in profile but the drapery is in frontal view. The unrealistic arrangement is like that seen on contemporary statues.[18] The fringe of the curved, proper right edge falls over the front of the robe along the proper right side of the body, ending just below knee level. The proper left side of the robe is also fringed and lies in part over the left shoulder, in part gathered in folds above and over the bent left arm. This fringed edge is at a higher level of relief than the rest of the garment. It ends in a curve at ankle-level. As on the statues, a puzzling extra flap of material descends at an angle from the left wrist and ends just below the calf with a straight fringed border. The top of the robe has a wide double band with rolled edge.

Behind the king stands a female figure facing left with bare arms bent up before her face in the typical pose of a minor goddess attending a worshiper on seals (Pl. 14a).[19] She wears a different type of dress than that of the deities already described, a long one that covers her left breast. Unlike the dress of the left-hand "angel" on register I, it has wide panels of small pleats clustered together like the sections of tufts on divine garments. The panels follow the curves of the body, suggesting that the gown was made of thin material. A heavy lock of wavy hair extends down her back and ends in a large curl at her waist. Another heavy lock cut off straight hangs over her chest.[20]

Farther to the right on the register a less well preserved, identically clad female figure faces right (**12** good face) behind a fragmentary figure of a king (**14**). This king is heavier than the other king but wears the same robe.[21] The fringed edges fall in identical fashion, suggesting that the missing proper left arm gathered the robe across the waist[22] while the missing proper right hand poured the libation. The king uses the same conical vessel to pour into a plant stand. The plant and stand are shorter and thicker than that at left.[23]

The stand rests on a wide double dias, the top stage shorter than the bottom. This dias extends to the edge of the stela. To the right of the stand is a god seated facing left on a throne in the shape of an entrance. Its perfect preservation allows a careful study of its details. It is a little shorter than the throne of the goddess.[24] The concave top slopes down slightly toward the front. The first, or outermost frame, which has a crook at either end, appears to be contiguous with the top.[25] From it hangs a row of scallops. The swags that hang across the third and fourth "door frames" may be intended to represent canopies over the deeper recesses of the door.[26] The inside edge of each "door jamb" is beveled down against the outside of the next, creating the illusion of recessed frames.

The god has a flat pillow under his feet. Over his left shoulder he holds, in his left hand, a short axe with a straight blade tilted downward towards the shaft. The shafthole is concave at the bottom and has a ridge along the top. In his right hand he holds out a coil of five strands of rope. The coil is held together by bands wrapped around at four intervals. The dangling ends of the strands are looped up, with three disappearing behind the long tapered pole held upright in the same hand.[27] The god's nails are suggested by small dents at the ends of the fingers. The rise of the

[18] Spycket p. 188.

[19] *PKG* 14, pl. 139a, h, k.

[20] The same figure occurs on a Gudea stela fragment, *BK* no. 89b. She is very similar to Akkadian-period goddesses from Susa: the one behind the kneeling figure of a god on a boulder of Puzur Inshushinak, Amiet, *L'art d'Agadé*, no. 33, p. 98 (= *Susa Cat.*, no. 54, pp. 88–90) and another on no. 34, p. 99.

[21] The curve of the buttocks, its surface completely eroded, is preserved on **12** good face and the lower part of the robe on **14**.

[22] Compare the upraised arm of the far left figure on register V, poor face (**28b**), where the fringe is erroneously shown along the outside of the gown.

[23] One wonders what the difference between the proportions of the figures and objects on the two sides of this scene means. Does it mean that the kings are two different people, the same king at different ages (as in Egyptian tomb statues), or merely that the carvers are not using a copy book? Note the position of the crescent over only one of the two kings in the top register of the poor face, which suggests that the kings are being differentiated.

[24] See Martin Metzger, *Königsthron*, pp. 152–154. He thinks the swags may be a hanging.

[25] Like the frame on the contemporary stela from Susa, *Susa Cat.*, no. 110 (= Moortgat, *Art*, fig. 210). This is unlike Šamaš's throne on the Hammurabi stela where the curved ends are on an extra top frame that would have made the seat more comfortable. Metzger, *Königsthron*, p. 154, suggests that on the Ur-Nammu stela we see the front face of the throne and that the side of the real throne would not have had the uncomfortable raised ends.

[26] These swags occur on an altar on the Gudea stela where the top is flat, *BK* nos. 81–84c.

[27] See Chapter 1, n. 66.

chest is shown under the garment. The biceps and deltoid of his bared upper right arm are indicated, as well
as the muscles along the inside of the lower arm. The
feet are carefully modeled.

The god has wavy locks of hair pulled back from
the brow and made into a braided bun behind the ear.
His beard is different from the king's. It is combed into five separate clusters of wavy strands with a curl at
the end of each. Unlike the beard of the king in register III below (**14**), it has no curls at the top. The crown
is identical to that of the goddess; its disc also is inter-
rupted by the dividing band. Unfortunately the small
fragment with the face of the god has been lost. It was
restored from a cast of the face of the god in the register below.[28] The god's robe differs from that of the
goddess only in having a separate flap of material that
covers his lower left arm. The tufts on this are twice as
long as those on the rest of the garment.[29]

"REGISTERS" III AND IV

On the right end of register III, standing on top of
a brick building,[30] a king carrying tools faces left behind a god also facing left who, to judge from the fact
that his head and shoulders are lower than the king's,
must be seated (**14**). The god raises his open right
hand in front of his nose in the usual Mesopotamian
gesture of homage.[31] The courtesy can hardly be addressed to the construction workers the god faces.[32] It
must be addressed to the structure itself, "raising its
head above" the plain, as Mesopotamian hymns say.
This is the same kind of anthropomorphizing heard in
hymns written to temples which can refer poetically to
details of construction.[33] A similar personification of
the structure itself is seen in earlier periods when liba-

tions are performed before temples (Pl. 16a).[34]

The god's face is the only perfectly preserved one
on the stela (Pl. 31). His eyebrows, carved in relief,
curve from the bridge of the nose to the temple. The
top of the heavy eyelid arches up toward the brow and
descends abruptly to the large tear duct. The nose is
straight and full with fleshy nostrils and rounded tip.
The full upper lip protrudes, suggesting a moustache,
but there is no incision visible. The long wavy beard is
combed into four wide clusters of tapering strands.
The hair is pulled back from the brow and gathered
into a plump bun behind the ear. The god wears the
same crown as the other deities but it is smaller. His
shoulders are also narrower. Once again the disc on
the crown is cut off by the divider.

Over his shoulder the king carries an axe with a
long handle. The blade, unlike the one in the register
above, is at right angles to the shaft. The blade is wider
at the straight cutting edge than at the shafthole.
Hung by a handle over the shaft is a conical basket
with a wide flat base. It is made of seven coils of twisted
material and resembles the basket carried on the head
of a workman directly below in register IV. Behind the
basket is a collapsed plow (Pls. 31–33).

The king's torso is well preserved. The corner of
his robe is visible here, tucked in over his right breast
as on contemporary statues.[35] He wears a necklace and
robe like those of the other royal figures on the stela
and a simple bracelet on each wrist. The brim of a
smooth round cap covers the upper part of his left ear.
A heavy lock of wavy hair with thin strands on top is visible beneath the brim, drawn back from the forehead
to the ear. Behind this on the nape of the neck are two
rows of tight curls (Pl. 32 detail and see *Frontispiece*).

Only on this fragment is the dressing of the king's

[28] The original face can be seen on *UE* VI, pl. 42d; the restored
face on pl. 43a (Pl. 3a, b here and see Pl. 32).

[29] This flap also appears on the Gudea stelae, when the arm is
bent, but not on the robe of a god whose arm is raised, e.g., *BK*
no. 35 (in Berlin). On the robes of the god on a stela from Susa
that probably belongs in the Ur III period, *Susa Cat.*, no. 111,
and on the later Hammurabi stela, *PKG* 14, pl. 181, the flaps lie
over the second tier of tufts.

[30] The sizes of the bricks vary slightly.

[31] "Hand to Nose" is the term used in the texts, see Winter 1987,
p. 192.

[32] Identified as workers by the length of their skirts, which is
proved by the bare legs of the figure before the king (**18**) and
the servant behind him (**20**).

[33] See Åke Sjöberg and E. Bergmann S.J., *The Collection of the
Sumerian Temple Hymns* (Locust Valley, NY, 1969), especially no.
1, line 12: "Your firmly jointed house"; no. 5, line 64: "Valiant?
brickwork"; no. 7, line 94: "your bricks are (well) moulded"; and
others. Also from the Kesh hymn, third millennium B.C.:

House Kesh, doorpost of the country
to Aratta a ferocious bull.
Grown (to vie) with the hills
embracing heaven,
house, grown (to vie) with the mountains,
lifting the head above the mountains,
opalescent like the deep,
green like the hills!"
. . . .
House, great corners thrust against the sky,
right good house, great side walls
thrust against the sky, house, great crown thrust against
    the sky . . .
                              (Jacobsen, *Harps*, pp. 379–380)

[34] On an Early Dynastic plaque from Ur, Winter 1987, fig. 2, p.
193 (= *Ur 'of the Chaldees'*, p. 125); on the Akkadian-period
plaque of Enheduanna, Winter 1987, fig. 1 (*Ur 'of the Chaldees'*, p.
127 = *PKG* 14, pl. 101).

[35] The tucked-in corner is also seen on the tall attendant with
towel in the wrestling scene on register IV, poor face (**29**).

beard completely preserved. It begins at the hairline with four rows of tight curls but does not continue over the lips like that of Ur Ningirsu from Tello.[36] The eight long twisted and tapered strands end in curls lined up straight. The king's collar bone appears above the necklace and his chest muscles are clearly rendered under the garment. Those along the bare inner right arm are also shown and the fingernails are indicated by notches.

The servant behind the king lightly touches the plow and basket with his fingertips, suggesting he is merely trying to stabilize them. Bald and bare-chested, he looks peculiar because his head is the same size as the king's and therefore too large for his shorter, slenderer body. He has a thick strap across his right shoulder and chest which goes under a wide double belt. The collar bone at the edge of the raised thorax and the channel between the biceps and triceps are clearly rendered. The sculptor seems to have experimented by showing the line of the proper left shoulder blade on the torso under the left arm (Pl. 32 detail). This exaggerates the "hunch-back" always created when an arm is extended across a frontal torso.

Facing the god is a figure who stands over a ladder leaning to the left against the building below (18).[37] His bare right leg is preserved to calf-level, proving his skirt was short. Behind him, also facing right, is another figure represented by the toe of a right foot (17). Beneath the toe is the left side of a second ladder that leans in the opposite direction. Still farther to the left, a figure kneels above the building (16). He holds something in the palm of his right, outstretched hand.[38] On a famous Akkadian seal, a god kneels over the top of a building in a similar fashion to catch or throw something.

At the righthand side of "register" IV below, a workman, hair combed forward in strands, faces left in front of the brick building, and carries a basket on his head (25). He raises both hands to grasp the rim between fingers and thumbs. Two coils at the bottom of the basket may be a separate wicker circlet used to soften or balance the load. Heaped high in the basket is a smooth material, probably ordinary mortar for the real building operation that seems to be pictured. Kings of Ur and Lagash usually carry baskets this way when represented as foundation figurines,[39] but theirs were undoubtedly heaped with the special ingredients mixed to make the first ceremonial brick (Pl. 16b).[40] To the left of the workman stand three more basket carriers, the farthest out at the foot of the ladder that leans to the left against the building (22–24).

Between the ladders is the entrance to the building. What remains is a fragment of the right side of the door with two recessed frames (21). The plane of the outer frame is 7 mm above that of the bricks to the right. The door would have been at least twice the surviving width but would still be too short for the figures in the scene to fit through. In this, it resembles the small doors on seals commonly used as a sort of pictograph for the whole building (Pl. 16a).[41] At the left side of the scene there is a structure with a sloping, plastered face that cuts across the brick wall (15). Leaning against it at the top of the register is a pole or ladder from which a curved "streamer"(?) waves.

REGISTER V

Under the brick building, a band 0.212 m high corresponds to the large panel of inscription on the opposite face of the stela (22). Immediately below this on register V are the tips of a pair of horns and the beginning of another pair to the right. These are more delicate than the tips of the crescent on the standards on register II, poor face (12 poor face), and could belong to animals.

---

[36] *PKG* 14, pl. 64.

[37] The top piece of this fragment was discovered in the first season, 1922–23, two years before the discovery of the large group of pieces. It was thought then to be a "scene of troops attacking a walled town" and dated to the reign of the "Chaldaean governor of Ur in the time of Ashur-bani-pal (668–626 B.C.)," see *AJ* III, p. 324 and pl. XXXIII (U.304).

[38] The thin edge of something held in the palm proves this is the

right hand. In my previous reconstruction in Canby 1987, p. 61, fig. 13, I took this hand to be the left.

[39] Ur-Nammu as foundation figurine: *PKG* 14, pl. 65.

[40] For a description of Gudea mixing the ingredients in a basket for the first ceremonial brick, see Jacobsen, *Harps*, pp. 410–412.

[41] Canby 1993, p. 148.

"POOR" FACE

REGISTER I

A goddess (an "angel," in Legrain's words), in pleated gown and two-horned crown floats in from the left (**1**). A wavy lock of hair lies along her back and another falls over her breast (Pl. 20 bottom). Her pleated dress spreads as it flows back. She holds a vessel like that held by the goddess on the opposite face—the round bottom supported in her right palm and the rim grasped by the left hand. Arching her back, she holds her head far above the streams which again undulate side to side and forward and back from the relief surface. Between the streams is the tip of a plant toward which a king to the right, standing facing left, extends his right arm to pour a libation. There is not enough space between the tree and the left edge of the stela for a seated figure under the flying goddess. I have instead restored a standing figure here, one like the frontal goddess on sealings from Nippur who stands on one side of a tree and extends a "Rod and Ring" toward a king pouring a libation on the other side (Pl. 14b).[42]

The king holds his balled left hand over his long beard which is twisted into seven strands, each with a curl at the end. He wears the usual round wide-brimmed cap, and a necklace with a large oval bead flanked by two round ones hanging on five thin strands. A peculiar raised area above the top edge of the gown was probably left for the border of the robe, which was never carved. His face is missing from cap to the tip of his nose. His upper lip protrudes immediately beneath the nose, but the cracked surface is too damaged to tell whether there was a moustache. The muscles of his bare right shoulder and upper arm are carefully modeled.

Back-to-back with the king is another royal figure, also with right arm extended (**8**). He stands before a seated deity now represented by only a tiny fragment of drapery (**10**). There is no room between the right-facing king and the seated deity for a plant on which to pour a libation. The king could be raising his hand before his face or he could be presenting something.

A large crescent in the field above is not centered between the kings but is instead clearly positioned over the head of the king at left.[43] As noted above (p. 9), it is not the custom to put a symbol over either king or god in Mesopotamian art. To place it over just one figure in a pair seems still more strange, and may have political overtones.[44] In any case, it further differentiates the two scenes at either side of the register and the scenes on each face of the top register.

REGISTER II

Only the right half of the register is preserved (**12** poor face). At left, two men are butchering a bovine that lies on its back, head at right. Something around the neck ends in a tassel. At right, a figure facing left, foot raised on the throat of the animal, pulls the front legs forward. Facing him, a bald, beardless man bends over, hands inside the animal, whose hind legs stretch out beyond him.[45] To the right of the butchers, facing the opposite direction, another bald, beardless figure leans forward pouring a thick stream of liquid from a headless male goat or skin-bag.[46] He holds the hind legs in his right hand and thrusts his left arm between the forelegs to grasp the neck (Pl. 29). All three figures wear a knee-length, wrap-around skirt fringed along the end. The hem rises in front above the bent knee.[47] Across their bare chests they wear a diagonal strap that ends in a double belt, like that of the servant behind the king in register III on the opposite face. The butchers have thick knives tucked in the lower belt. To the right of these three figures, a very small, nude figure stands on a two-stepped pedestal. In his right

---

[42] Dating to Amar-Sin, B. Buchanan, "An Extraordinary Seal Impression of the Third Dynasty of Ur," *JNES* 31 (1972), pp. 96–101; idem., *Early Near Eastern Seals in the Yale Babylonian Collection*, no. 681, pp. 262–263; R. Zettler, *JNES* 46 (1987), p. 60 with new drawing. On the seal, see I. Winter, "Legitimation and Authority through Image and Legend," *The Organization of Power, Studies in Ancient Oriental Civilizations* 46 (Chicago, 1987), p. 78, pls. 9b, c, 10a.

[43] The chip with the top of the king's cap over which is an edge of the crescent was found in storage at an early stage (Canby 1987, Canby 1998) and attached.

[44] See n. 23 above on the difference between the figures of the king in register II, good face.

[45] See the similar scene on an Akkadian seal, Amiet, *L'art d'Agadé*, no. 80 (= Frankfort, *CS*, pl. XXIII, f).

[46] The fact that the legs and genitals of the animal are shown has led some to the conclusion the animal is about to be cut up for meat, i.e., Woolley, *UE* VI, p. 78, n. 118. However, skin-bags with the legs still on do occur. A copy of one in silver was found in the Ur graves, see M. Müller-Karpe, Metallgefässe im Iraq I, *Prähistorische Bronzefunde* II, 14 (Stuttgart, 1993), no. 1489; *Sumerian Art Illustrated by Objects from Ur and Ubaid* (London: British Museum, 1969), pl. XVId (B.M. 121449).

[47] That the angle of the hem on the righthand butcher is not created by his raised leg is demonstrated by the hemline of the pouring figure, which is similarly raised although he does not raise his leg.

hand he holds a rod or stick from the top of which another rod projects downward. This has been interpreted as a flail, flute, or hoe.[48]

After a small gap there is a unique scene that is, unfortunately, badly damaged. Legrain suggested we see emblems at the entrance to a shrine and a sacred wood.[49] Woolley hesitantly suggested that the objects at the right might be the wall of a byre.[50] Actually, what we see here is a row of standards, similar to but much longer than ones on a Gudea stela.[51] In front of these there is a chariot.[52] Traces of the latter consist of reins passing through two rings which can be seen beneath the third standard from the left (as viewed). Below the rein rings is a small stretch of the back of the draft animal. The line of the reins, which follows the arched draft pole joining the animal to the chariot (now missing) to the right, can be traced to the beginning of its curved downward return abutting the seventh standard. Here a diagonal projection could represent the quiver often carried on the front of chariots. A quiver-like projection occurs on a worn fragment found in storage showing an elaborate chariot (73). Unfortunately, this area has so many stone chips missing that it is now impossible to be sure this very elaborate version with rampant animals above the handrail fitted here.[53] A fragment of a wheel in good condition, also found in storage (13), may belong to the chariot on the stela.

Above the chariot we see a row of standards comprising nine vertical poles, some with objects attached to them (12). None of the tops are fully preserved. The empty space still preserved to the left of the row suggests that it begins here. I describe each standard, counting from the left (Pl. 30).

The first standard has a crescent across it. It and the second emerge from a high, rectangular base, which has curved elements carved on the face. The third and fourth standards are very worn but the bottom of the fourth can be seen on top of the arched reins. The fifth standard, which also is seen above the reins, touches a lower rounded element on the sixth standard. This is a badly damaged, raised area on which some curved and V-shaped incisions can be seen. Above it is another rounded element that curves out on either side. Standard seven, which also touches the edge of the lower element on the sixth, ends against the reins. The surface between standard seven and standard eight is concave. A tiny well-preserved fragment from storage preserved the top end of the seventh standard and a rounded protrusion on either side of standard eight. Because the edges of the protrusion are chipped and pocked, its original shape is uncertain. The top of the ninth standard flares out on either side. Farther down it is crossed by a curved object with several attachments(?) that vaguely resembles a bull's head, but the surface of this whole raised area is lost. Some of the depressions may actually be edges of relief and not pock marks, because the stone here appears to be uniformly fine-grained without inclusions. Traces of more standards to the right suggest the row continues to the right edge of the stela.

REGISTER III

At the lefthand side, a figure is seated facing right on a stool set on an unusual podium (28a). It is twice as high as the dias under the deities in register II, good face, and lifts the person well above the scene before him. There are three small steps at the top.[54] The back is lost. The feet of the stool are badly damaged but the rung makes its identity certain. It is the type covered with three tiers of fleece tufts that was introduced in the Ur III period. Used occasionally by deities, it is mostly seen under kings in scenes in which a person is presented to him as if to a god (Pl. 14c).[55] As seen there, kings sometimes even wear a divinity's tufted robe.[56] The humble seat, which occurs on the stela only here, surely identifies the seated figure as the king. The feet rest on a thin, flat pillow similar to the god's on register II of the opposite face.

At the foot of the dais, back turned to the king, stands a bald, beardless figure in a long fringed robe. His lowered arms meet, hands holding a straight thin

[48] Legrain, MJ 18, p. 89, quotes Woolley who thought this was a statue. See A. Spycket, "Les statues de culte" (1968), p. 60.

[49] See MJ 18, p. 89; RA XXX, p. 115.

[50] See UE VI, p. 78, where Woolley also discussed the fragment with the legs of a person followed, perhaps, by an animal (catalogue no. 46), which was arbitrarily restored at the right of the scene.

[51] BK no. 63 (= PKG 14, pl. 110a).

[52] In this connection, note that a goddess tells Gudea to erect in the temple a mace and standard as well as an elegant chariot if

he wants to understand the god's wishes (Jacobsen, Harps, p. 396).

[53] Gods as well as kings had chariots. They had numerous roles in Sumerian art, see M. Civil, "Išme-Dagan and Enlil's Chariot," Journal of the American Oriental Society 88 (1968), pp. 3–7.

[54] There is a deity on a plain (or worn) throne on a similar high multi-stepped dais from Tello, Louvre A.O. 27, unpublished.

[55] Porada, PM, p. 35. I. Winter (1986, pp. 253–268) studies this subject in detail. Metzger, Königsthrön, pp. 159ff.

[56] PKG 14, pl. 139g.

object that touches the thigh of a figure facing right in front of him. The latter is dressed in a wrap-around skirt with a triple belt that ends in a tuft at the waist. Two faint ridges running diagonally forward from the waist mark the edge of the wrap. The surface is too worn to be able to tell if it was fringed. It is also impossible to tell the length of the skirt because the edges of the lower part of the figure are badly broken. The surface is lost from mid-thigh down and there are no good edges along the hollow between the legs.

Woolley thought the bald figure was holding a rope attached to a prisoner in front of him and that the prisoner had his hands tied behind him. Legrain also interpreted this figure as a prisoner but thought Woolley's "rope" was a baton.[57] In fact, the prisoner's "hands" are actually the short tuft on his skirt.

This thin straight object probably is a kind of baton but not one used by guards. Instead, I think it is the baton used by referees such as those seen beside Sumerian, ancient Egyptian, and later Etruscan wrestling matches.[58] The "prisoner" would be a clothed wrestler who is involved, along with the referee, in some sort of ceremony prior to the match in register IV. Referees and clothed wrestlers appear in a procession in conjunction with a wrestling match on a stela of the Early Dynastic period from Badra, where wrestlers without skirts also kneel (Pl. 14d). All that remains of the right side of this register is a liquid, falling and spreading over the top of the divider in undulating waves (29).

REGISTER IV

On the left, bearded men stand on either side of an enormous drum, beating it in turn (28a). The man at the left supports the drum with his left hand and strikes it with his right. The taller man at right supports the drum with his right hand and has his left

hand up, ready to strike. The head of the right drummer is relatively well preserved with the eye still visible (Pl. 39, detail). His hair is combed forward over the ears and brow, and his pointed beard is arranged in rows of curls. He wears a long, pleated skirt with a wide belt. It splits and exposes the leading leg below the knee, but the surface is too damaged to see whether he had a short skirt underneath similar to that of one of Gudea's drummers.[59] Behind the right drummer stands another, badly damaged, bearded figure. The traces suggest that he had his arms raised. Unlike the drummers, his long robe covers his leading leg. A drum with a wrestler dancing on top of it occurs on the Badra stela, mentioned above (Pl. 14d).[60]

The unique scene on the right side of this register (29) has been variously interpreted. Legrain, followed hesitantly by Woolley, thought it might show someone carrying a dead body. More recently, Börker-Klähn has suggested that it pictures the king bathing.[61] Certain details indicate it actually represents a wrestling match, a sport well attested in this period.[62]

There are two groups of figures. At left, a tall figure in a long robe is bald and beardless with a long, thin nose and an ear set far up on the back of the head. He faces left; with the tip of his cupped left hand he touches the beard of a figure stooping in front of him. A long fringed cloth hangs over the tall figure's extended left arm, hiding his right lower arm and hand. His robe is gathered back over the crook of his left arm with fringed edge shown hanging down on both sides of the arm in an unusual fashion. There is no trace of the flap seen on royal robes. The other end of the robe is tucked in the top of the gown below the right shoulder.

The stooping figure has a short pointed beard and his thick hair falls forward from the crown ending in a series of small curls around the face and neck (Pl. 43).

---

[57] For these opinions, see *UE* VI, p. 78.

[58] For the referee's baton, see the plaque from Sin Temple, Khafaje (Pl. 15a), J. Boese, "Ringkampf-Darstellung in Frühdynastischer Zeit," *AfO* 22 (1968/69), p. 35, fig. 7; idem, "Altmesopotamische Weihplatten," *Untersuchungen zur Assyriologie und vorderasiatischen Archäologie* 6 (Berlin, 1971), pl. IX, below; *Der Garten in Eden Jahrtausende Kunst und Kultur an Euphrat und Tigris*, Baghdad exh. cat. (Berlin, 1978), no. 67; also the staffs of the referees on the Badra stela, *BK* nos. 12a–d; F. Safar, *Sumer* (1971), pp. 15–24; S. A. Rashid, *Sumer* (1975), pp. 39ff. Batons were also used in wrestling matches in ancient Egypt, see A. D. Touny and S. Wenig, *Sport in Ancient Egypt* (Leipzig, 1969), pg. 21. For Etruria, see K. Vellucci, "Etruscan Athletics," *Exp* 77 (1985), p. 23, fig. 2, Tomb of the Augurs. S. Steingräber, *Catalogo Regionato della Pittura Etrusca* (1985), no. 42, p. 289, color pl. 18.

On the Khafajah plaque, one of the wrestlers is bald, one bearded; on the Badra stela, there is a procession of bald, clean-shaven figures meeting one of long-haired bearded figures. Probably they are members of the two teams, but unfortunately only one bald head of the figures actually wrestling survives.

[59] *BK* nos. 45b, 64, 79.

[60] See also the figure on top of an enormous drum carved in relief on the side of a bowl in the Louvre, Moortgat, *Art*, fig. 200.

[61] "Šulgi Badet," *ZA* 64 (1965), pp. 233ff.

[62] For wrestling texts: recently, J. Klein, "A Self-Laudatory Šulgi Hymn from Nippur," *The Tablet and the Scroll: Near Eastern Studies in Honor of William W. Hallo* (Bethesda, MD: CDL Press, 1993), p. 126; see also Å. Sjöberg, "Trials of Strength," *Exp* 27 (1985), pp. 7–9.

His proper left shoulder is hunched as he twists his left arm around the buttocks of a figure who faces in the opposite direction in front of him. The back of the head of the second figure and his muscular left upper arm, bent at the elbow, are visible along the break. At waist-level between the arms of the figures are three ridges of a typical Mesopotamian wrestling belt. This type of belt is customarily seen on the Mesopotamian hero or bull-man struggling with animals or with other heroes. It appears in art from the Protoliterate period on but it is best known from contest scenes on Akkadian seals. Figurines of nude wrestlers with belts also occur in Early Dynastic times.[63] The fragment (30) that preserves the crease between an arm pressed against a buttock in the reconstruction was located in storage and may belong here.

The wrestling hold is reconstructed loosely on the basis of that on the lower register of an Early Dynastic plaque from the Nintu temple at Khafaje, dating to the mid-third millennium B.C. (Pl. 15b, c).[64] There, a bearded figure whose right leg is pulled up by his opponent (whose head is missing) leans forward, clenching his hands around the opponent's buttocks. The latter leans forward to reach around the bearded figure's neck and across his chest to pin his left arm.

At right, standing on a plain platform higher than normal but less high than the king's in register III above, a small nude figure faces a seated deity who has a flat pillow under his feet. With his left hand, the nude figure waves a "whisk" in front of the deity. A raised area along the break beyond the tip of the whisk may be the edge of the crown.[65] The nude figure holds over the palm of his right hand a long cloth

fringed at both ends. A thin raised edge along the break at elbow level suggests that the deity's arm was bent across the waist. The deity is apparently merely observing the match without making any participatory gesture such as those made by the deities on register II of the opposite face.

A dais of the same unusual height as the deity's is preserved on a corner fragment (31), which is restored here as the probable end of this scene. The dais terminates short of the right edge of the stela, in the same way as the dais under the goddess in register II, good face, which might suggest the deity here is also feminine.

Another wrestler(?) (32–34) probably belongs somewhere in this scene. He is dressed in a short skirt with a tuft at the back, like the figure before the referee in register III above. Such tufted skirts are worn by the bald wrestlers in groups of contestants on the Badra stela (Pl. 14d). The curve of the hip below the high waist and the diagonal edge of the skirt-fringe suggest that he is leaning forward, perhaps with right leg raised (see Pl. 44).[66] On the torso fragment of this figure (32), the elbow is bent. The arm is unusually thick.

It seems probable to me that the scenes on registers III and IV should be interpreted as a single episode which, like the activities at the building site on the opposite face, occupies two registers.[67] The central event is a wrestling match accompanied by drums. It is preceded by some sort of ceremony involving referee and clothed contestant(s?) and is observed by a king and a deity seated high above the combatants on opposite sides of the "ring."

[63] Protoliterate examples of wrestling belt and figures: *PKG* 14, pls. 72, 73. Early Dynastic statuettes: a kneeling wrestler in stone with a five-ridged belt from the hoard of statues at Tell Asmar, H. Frankfort, Sculpture from the 3rd Millennium B.C. from Tell Asmar and Khafajah, *Oriental Institute Publications* 44 (Chicago, 1939), no. 16 (see in the group photograph, Frankfort, *A and A*, pl. 13, bottom row second from right); a similar figure from Agrab carries a pot, H. Frankfort, More Sculpture from the Diyala Region, *Oriental Institute Publications* 60 (Chicago, 1943), no. 269, pls. 33, 34 (= *PKG* 14, pl. 36a); a bull-man with triple belt from Umma, *PKG* 14, pl. 16; a kneeling figure with belt from Isin should probably be added, B. Hrouda et al., *Isin-Isan Bahriyat III, Ergebnisse der Ausgrabungen 1983/84* (Munich, 1987), p. 61, pl. 25.

There is also an Early Dynastic bronze group of wrestling figures, arms grasping each other's belts: *PKG* 14, pl. 35 (= Frankfort, *A and A*, pl. 20c); bronze nude with belt, ibid., pl. 39a (= Frankfort, *A and A*, pl. 20b); also see the wrestling scene on the Badra stela and plaque from Khafaje, n. 58 above.

For the tripartite belt usually worn by the bull-man on Akkadian seals, see good examples in *PKG* 14, pl. 134a, c, e–g, j; for the same worn by the hero wrestling a lion, ibid., pl. 135a, b; for the lower half of an Akkadian bronze life-size figure seated in a

twisted position on the ground, from Bassetki in Iraqi Kurdistan: A. H. Fouadi, "The Bassetki Statue with an Old Akkadian Royal Inscription of Naram-Sin of Agade, B.C. 2291–2255," *Sumer* 32 (1976), p. 63; W. Farber, "Die Vergöttlichung Naram-Sins," *Orientalia* 52 (1983), pp. 67–72; E. Braun-Holzinger, Figürliche Bronzen aus Mesopotamien, *Prähistorische Bronzefunde*, !:4 (Munich, 1984), no. 61, pl. 23, pl. 13; B. Brentjes, "Terrakotta und Grossplastik in Altvorderasien," *Beschreiben und Deuten, Festschrift für Ruth Mayer-Opificius* (Munster, 1994), p. 17.

[64] *PKG* 14, fig. 81a; Moortgat, *Art*, fig. 38.

[65] The crown is not preserved, *pace* Woolley, *UE* VI, p. 79.

[66] The thighs of the Nintu wrestlers and of the wrestlers on the Badra stela are also unusually thick. Ancient Greek wrestlers were also heavy, see W. Decker, *Sport in der griechischen Antike* (Munich: C.H. Beck, 1995), p. 81, fig. 26. One is reminded of the very heavy Japanese sumo wrestlers and American "professional" wrestlers.

[67] Legrain, quoted by Woolley, *UE* VI, p. 79, called attention to the similarity between the figures seated on high platforms and thought they marked either end of a scene. This agrees with my understanding of the composition, except that the wrestlers,

INSCRIPTION

A panel 22.0 cm high with an inscription (see Appendix 1) comes between registers IV and V.[68] It is written in two "columns," lying horizontally on the stone, and has incised lines ("cases") marking out the sections. The inscription begins in the upper right corner as it is laid out in the panel of the stela. On the lower left edge of the inscription as viewed on the stela, on **28b** (which is the end of column II when the inscription was read), the signs were erased, leaving only fragments of two signs.[69] Pressure marks from the case frames which once outlined the signs are visible on the lowered surface in this area. The lower column (II) is much damaged. There are legible signs on **28a**, and two signs on **28d**.[70] Farther still to the right, **28c** has four cases of the lower column (II) partly preserved together with a small, broken section of the upper one (I).[71] There is a section of the right side of the wide panel preserved (on **66a, b**), but there are no traces of inscription.

REGISTER V

At the left stands a bald and clean-shaven attendant (**28b**), taller than any of the non-royal figures on the stela except the servant behind the king on register III, good face. He raises clasped hands to his face in an exceptional gesture. Hands are normally lifted separately in gestures of respect (Pls. 14a, 25).[72] The sculptor had difficulty with the pose. Instead of placing the proper left upper arm outside the torso, he lined it up with the hips.[73] The robe is pulled over the proper left shoulder and falls in folds above the crook of that arm. The fringed edge is shown hanging along the

outside of the gown, as is usual when a figure facing right has the proper left arm extended.

In front of the worshiper stands a king facing right (**28b**). The figure is badly damaged but the outline implies his hands were clasped over his waist in a familiar gesture.[74] He faces a plain, empty, rectangular altar on the other side of which an attendant, facing left, holds up a traditional high-footed vessel in both hands. The libator wears a long robe or skirt. Most of the elements of the scene are familiar but the arrangement of figures is unusual. Woolley thought that the king was watching the libation, but if that were the case, he should stand behind the libator.[75] Legrain believed that the royal figure was being worshiped, but that it was a statue, perhaps a figure of Ur-Nammu set up by his son Šulgi.[76] However, if the worshiper standing behind it to the left means the figure does not, like a statue, stand against a wall, the royal figure may represent a living king. Worship of kings occurred during the Third Dynasty of Ur when living kings, with the exception of Ur-Nammu, were deified.[77]

Behind the libator there is the top of a plant like the one over which a king pours a libation three times elsewhere on the stela. There is a gap between the plant and the piece that preserves the upper right side of the register. Here there is a row of seven symbols like those above the chariot in register II above. On the left is the trace of an object tapering upward. Then come a crescent, a flat-topped pole, a second crescent, a sphere on a short collar above something with a wide concave top, a third crescent with a flattened curve at the bottom, and then a fourth, normal crescent on a pole or collar. The tight spacing is like that in register II. Tips of horns also occur in register V on the opposite face, but they are more broadly spaced.

---

because of space constraints, must be placed in register IV, a register lower than where he had placed them, see Chapter 2.

[68] For inscriptions, see *UET* I, no. 44(b), p. 9, pls. 8, 9; *MJ* 18, pp. 88, 89, 91–93; *UE* VI, p. 79, pls. 41b, 4c.

[69] These are just visible on the photograph in *UE* VI, pl. 44c (= *MJ* 18, p. 92). The isolated traces are very difficult to see and were probably not noticed. They are not mentioned in the Ur publications, see Pl. 60 here.

[70] *UET* I, no. 44(b), fragments 1, 3.

[71] *UET* I, no. 44(b), fragment 2.

[72] Like those of the goddesses on register II, good face.

[73] The proper left upper arm of the typical goddess with upraised hands is conventionally covered either by the other arm or by the fringes of her robe. The same pose as the worshiper here, and a similar solution to the difficulty it causes, can be seen on the relief, said to have come from Ur, in the *Ladders to Heaven*

collection, *PKG* 14, fig. 116a. The rather crude carving of the latter piece and the gross facial features are quite unlike those seen on the Ur-Nammu stela or any head from the Gudea stelae.

[74] Not necessarily holding something as Woolley thought, *UE* VI, p. 79: see Gudea on his stelae, *BK* nos. 75, 81b. The pose also occurs on numerous seals.

[75] *UE* VI, p. 79, referring to the Early Dynastic plaque (Pl. 16a), *UE* IV, pl. 39 (= *Ur 'of the Chaldees'*, p. 125) and the plaque of Sargon's daughter, *UE* IV, pl. 41 (= Moorey, p. 127). On these pieces, figures stand behind the nude priest who pours a libation from the same type of vessel as that used on the stela.

[76] *MJ* 18, pp. 94, 95.

[77] For a recent explanation of the deification of kings in this period, see P. Michalowski, "Charisma and Control," in *The Organization of Power: Aspects of Bureaucracy in the Ancient Near East* (Chicago: Oriental Institute of the University of Chicago, 1987), pp. 65–68.

Standards, free-standing or carried by someone, are well known in Mesopotamia from very early times. On one of the Gudea stelae, four upright maces are lined up beside a standard topped by seven spheres, and all of these seem to be repeated on the other side of a blank stela represented there.[78] Another fragment shows a row of three men carrying standards.[79] However, I know of no representation of such long rows as those on the Ur Nammu stela. Nine standards are mentioned among weaponry in Gudea cylinder B.[80] The convex shape under the sphere is also unfamiliar. Could it be the top of a parasol like the one carried behind the king on an Akkadian stela?[81] Actually, the closest parallel may be the object carved on dense gray stone found here with the Ur Nammu fragments, **B1** (Pl. 61; Appendix 3).

---

[78] *BK* no. 63 a–b.

[79] *BK* no. 68.

[80] Jacobsen, *Harps*, p. 437 = Cylinder B, xiv.1.

[81] Amiet, *L'art d'Agadé*, p. 8, fig. 1, p. 73, lc = *PKG* 14, pl. 99a and b = *Susa Cat.*, fig. 46.

CHAPTER 4

Catalogue of Fragments Restored on the Stela

INTRODUCTION

Catalogue numbers

The University of Pennsylvania Museum accession number for all the pieces of the Ur-Nammu stela is CBS 16676. The separate pieces received individual numbers after the general number and a period, e.g., CBS 16676.1. Many of these pieces are themselves made up of fragments joined by Woolley or by me. Three pieces are made up of fragments known to have had important separate histories; in these cases each piece was given one suffix number with the individual fragments labeled alphabetically, e.g., CBS 16676.14a–f, 28a–d, and 66a, b. Throughout this publication, pieces are catalogued by the unique suffix number in bold-face type, dropping the CBS 16676 prefix.

A few of the pieces of the stela were given Ur excavation numbers (U.——) by Woolley, and these numbers are included in the catalogue.[1]

Placement

If a piece is in the reconstruction of the stela on paper (Pls. 10, 11), its location there is given in the catalogue. If followed by "?" the fragment does not join but is thought to be from the same scene. If it had been in a former reconstruction, that information is provided after the heading "Formerly." "From storage" indicates that the piece was found in the storage areas of the University of Pennsylvania Museum, labeled "Ur-Nammu stela."

The two faces of the stela are here labeled "good" and "poor." The terms reflect the general condition of the surface on that face, a surface that may vary in places. The terms replace "obverse" (= "good") and "reverse" (= "poor") for the faces, for which there was no evidence. Only two pieces, **1** and **12**, have both faces preserved, and each face is described separately under the headings "good" and "poor" face.

Description and condition, definition of terms used

"flake": a fragment detached in a thin slice along a

bedding plane
"chip": a fragment detached in a large or small chunk
"pocked": containing round holes left by loss of small pebbles or fossils
"worn": abraded
"dissolved": worn by water
"crisp": clean, sharp

Stone

The stone is pinkish buff in color and mostly fine grained. In places, fossils or small stones remain or, more often, pocks where they once were. Breaks seem to be along vertical bedding planes, but some very flat breaks (i.e., **14**, **28**) are perpendicular to bedding planes (Pls. 8b, 9a). There is sometimes a rusty stain, especially along crevices and pocks. (This staining also occurs on some of the fragments from other stelae, see Appendix 3.)

Bitumen and salt deposits

Bitumen is a naturally occurring adhesive found in Iraq (ancient Mesopotamia) that was used by ancient builders to waterproof or adhere an object or architectural member. If these things burned, the bitumen melted and could drip on objects below. Here the description of the bitumen accumulation on the fragments is supplied in order to illustrate something of their history. If bitumen occurs on a broken surface on the bottom of a fragment, it dripped when the block was upside down; if on the broken top, when the block was broken, but upright; if on both broken surfaces, the dripping occurred on two different occasions after it was broken, and so on.

Sampling

In December 1990, core samples (ca. 0.025 × 0.025 m) of the large blocks were taken to be sure they all came from the same stone, which proved to be the

---

[1] In two cases U. numbers were given to photographs! One of these, U.3329, comprises the pieces (one of which had separately received the number U.305 [see **18** here]) restored into an early reconstruction of the building scene and published as b on *UE* VI, pl. 43. The other, U.3330, was given to the 17 fragments published on ibid., pls. 43A and B.

case. In May 1991, samples were taken of the fragments carved from stone that did not look the same as that of the Ur-Nammu stela (Appendix 3). (They were compared to additional small samples taken in 1994 from the core holes previously made in the large blocks.) In 1992, a groove 0.01 m wide, 0.01 m deep was polished across the broken surface of the bottom of the "angel" block, **1**, to ascertain the stratigraphy of the stone. A thin slice along this groove was taken in 1994 in order to make a new acetate peel for examination. All these projects were supervised by Dr. Robert Giegengack (now Chair of Department of Earth and Environmental Science, University of Pennsylvania). No conclusions have been reached from the latter two studies except that the fragment with Ur-Nammu's name on it, **D1**, is carved from a different stone than that of the stela (pers. comm., R. Giegengack, May 31, 1994).

Findspots

These are based primarily on Woolley's attributions in the catalogue in *UE* VI, pp. 88, 96–98. Locations abbreviated there are followed by "=" and the location given for that abbreviation in a list in Museum archives. I have assumed that pieces "from storage" were part of the large group of fragments found on the southwest court of the Dublalmakh (see Chapter 1, p. 2).

Dimensions

"GPW," "GPH," "GPTh" signify greatest preserved width, height, and thickness, respectively.

Publication

The list of references includes only publication of the fragments by the members of the expedition to Ur or by me. It does not include all citations.

CATALOGUE

1 "ANGELS" AND KINGS   U.3266
1 good face, register I
Pls. 17, 18
1 poor face, register I
Pls. 7a, 19–21
Formerly register I, both faces

GENERAL CONDITION Natural cracks along and perpendicular to bedding planes; surfaces flaked and still flaking; small section of side face completely preserved. Bitumen drips on side face 0.12 m above bottom break. Unrecorded repairs in field before photography; no record of findspot of detached fragments; break at top trimmed for 1927 reconstruction of crescent (joining chips in plaster drips inside reconstruction).

1 good face: Surface partially preserved on part of king's brow, beard, robe, arm, "angel's" face, dress above left arm; "angel's" cheek, king's nose worn flat; chipping along king's proper right side, upper arms; larger chips above relief; "angel's" lower body on two separate fragments with well-worn, salt-covered breaks between. Bitumen drips extending from bottom break up to sections of vessel, water, "angel's" dress (i.e., deposited when block upside down, but before dress fragment had been separated from the main block); bitumen extending down from top break on good surface in front of king, on broken surface before "angel" (i.e., deposited when block upright, after surface damaged). Sliver of surface with supposed "outline of crescent"(?) mentioned by Woolley above king's head, lost (Pl. 18 top).[2]

1 poor face: Thin chip with king's turban,[3] thick fragment with crescent section, both found in storage. Surface partially preserved on background, water, "angel's" dress and crown, king's torso; "angel's" eye socket, back of lid, bridge of nose, thumb and fingers on left hand still clear; outline of parts of second king and three small sections of crescent preserved. Extensive flaking and chipping on upper left quadrant; "angel" and vessel entirely detached from main block in three fragments; gap up to 0.03 m wide (Pl. 7a), large chipped areas filled in at Ur with wax, plaster before photography.

SAMPLING 1990, core sample 0.025 × 0.025 m, taken from top break; 1994, core hole resampled; 1992, groove polished across and along bottom break from

---

[2] Woolley described (*UE* VI, pp. 76ff.) a "protuberance of stone the fragmentary outline of which is sufficient to identify it as a crescent carved in relief" directly above the king's head. That protuberance is now missing. A segment with a crack above the head of the king is visible in a photograph of the piece propped up on a basket at Ur (Pl. 18 top) of which *UE* VI, pl. 42b (= *AJ* V, pl. XLVI, 2) is a cropped version. That segment was missing by the time the piece was published in *MJ* 18, p. 74 (= *UE* VI, pl. 43a) but the curved line at the bottom of it was believed to be the

edge of the crescent in the 1927 restoration. Actually the line seems to be a crack rather than a protuberance because it casts no shadow. The edge of the crescent must have been outside the preserved edge of the relief.

[3] Canby 1987, p. 57, fig. 6c. The crisp condition of the fragile piece with the king's turban, which makes a tight join to the main fragment, suggests it was not in situ when excavated or Woolley would surely have joined it.

tree tip on poor face to king's forearm on good face; 1994, thin groove along same strip to examine stratigraphy of stone.

FINDSPOT *UE* VI, p. 97: "Filling of Lower Courtyard L.L." = "Dub-lal-mah"; no record of findspots of reattached fragments

DIMENSIONS Entire block, GPW 0.74; GPH 0.536; GPTh 0.28 m. Relief, GPW good face 0.54; GPH good face 0.392; GPW poor face 0.652; GPH poor face 0.50 m

PUBLICATION Good face: *AJ* V, pl. XLVI, 2, opp. p. 39, p. 399; *MJ* 18, pp. 74, 77, 80, 83; *UE* VI, pls. 41a, 42b; Canby 1987, p. 54, fig. 1, p. 58, fig. 7 b; Canby 1998, p. 45, fig. 10.

Poor face: *MJ* 18, p. 76; *UE* VI, pls. 41b, 42a; Canby 1987, p. 58, fig. 7 a, p. 59, fig. 8; Canby 1998, p. 45, fig. 11, p. 46, fig. 12, p. 48, fig. 14 top right

2 HAIR AND CROWN OF GOD U.2917[4]
Register I, good face?
Pl. 22
From storage

CONDITION Fine-grained surface, well preserved. One small drop bitumen on back edge of hair bun, two drops on top break; two small, thick patches of salt on back edge of top break. U. number written on back, 7 very light.

FINDSPOT ES = "Dub-lal-mah, building S of main court"

DIMENSIONS GPW 0.07; GPH 0.09; GPTh 0.025 m

PUBLICATION *UE* VI, pl. 43A.d, turned sideways; Canby 1987, p. 57, fig. 6 a, p. 59, fig. 8; Canby 1998, p. 46, fig. 12, p. 48, fig. 14 top left

3 HAND ON SHOULDER OF GOD
Register I, good face?
Pl. 22
From storage

CONDITION Three joining fragments, two joined before 1986; fine-grained stone; right edge of figure, part of garment, hand well preserved; other surfaces damaged and worn; all breaks worn except crisp back. No bitumen or salts.

DIMENSIONS GPW 0.11; GPH 0.155; GPTh 0.02 m

PUBLICATION *UE* VI, pl. 43B.b (lower arm); Canby 1987, p. 57, fig. 6, p. 59, fig. 8; Canby 1998, p. 46, fig. 12, p. 48, fig. 14 lower left

4 ARM WITH WATER BEHIND
Register I, good face?
Pl. 22
Formerly register I, "obverse"

CONDITION Two joining fragments of fine-grained stone, broken subsequent to first photograph(?)[5]; surface for the most part well preserved; breaks old and worn except for small areas on back. No bitumen or salts.

DIMENSIONS GPW 0.05; GPH 0.17; GPTh 0.04 m

PUBLICATION *MJ* 18, pp. 80, 82; *UE* VI, p. 76, pls. 41a, 45c; Canby 1987, p. 59, fig. 8; Canby 1998, p. 46, fig. 12

5 PART OF "ANGEL'S" GOWN AND SIDE FACE OF TOP REGISTER
Register I, good face
Pl. 23
Formerly register I, "obverse"

CONDITION Fine-grained stone, worn with a few small pocks; all breaks old. One small bitumen drop on front; no salts.

DIMENSIONS GPW 0.15; GPH 0.23; GPTh 0.04 m

PUBLICATION *UE* VI, p. 76, pl. 41a

6 CRESCENT AND STAR[6]
Register I, good face
Pl. 23
Formerly register I, "obverse"

CONDITION Three long-separated fragments; very worn with thick salt deposits on breaks; surface of background well preserved; parts of relief elements chipped off; slightly convex side face preserved in part, roughly finished. Some bitumen bits; one small salt deposit on relief face. In 1927 edge of side face trimmed and covered with plaster, presumably to make piece fit restored curvature of monument.

DIMENSIONS GPW 0.35; GPH 0.19; GPTh 0.225 m

PUBLICATION *UE* VI, pl. 41a

7 STAR POINT
Register I, good face?
Pl. 24
From storage

DESCRIPTION Double incised line inside raised star point; same size as those on sun-disc on stela.

CONDITION Surface in part well preserved; breaks worn. Overall thin white (salt?) film; side breaks covered with salts; no bitumen.

DIMENSIONS GPW 0.08; GPH 0.04; GPTh 0.11 m

---

[4] U.2917 in field catalogue reads: "Relief of human figure and other objects."

[5] The break is not visible in *UE* VI, pl. 45c.

[6] Legrain erroneously (see below, entry for **35**) claimed this piece (**6**) joined the other face; *RA* XXX, p. 114.

8 NECK AND SHOULDER OF LARGE-SCALE KING

Register I, poor face?

Pl. 24

Formerly under plaster in 1927 restoration of king at right, register II, "obverse"

CONDITION   Relief surface slightly worn; side breaks dissolved; right break flat. Bitumen drop on top, right break, beard; salts on neck.

DIMENSIONS   GPW 0.06; GPH 0.06; GPTh 0.045 m

PUBLICATION   *UE* VI, pls. 41a, 43a

9 PART OF LARGE-SCALE KING'S ROBE

Register I, poor face?

Pl. 24

From storage

DESCRIPTION   Narrow slice of robe extending from proper left side of a standing figure facing left to the vertical fringe; width suggests from large figure, immediately below a bent arm; cf. left-hand king, register II, good face.

CONDITION   Surface well preserved; breaks worn except at bottom. Two bitumen drips on relief surface, one on the face from top to right break; salt speck on surface.

DIMENSIONS   GPW 0.07; GPH 0.015; GPTh 0.06 m

10 PART OF LARGE-SCALE DIVINE ROBE

Register I, poor face?

Pl. 24

From storage

DESCRIPTION   Flake of drapery from waist of seated deity; length of tufts below triangle at waist suggests figure facing left;[7] raised area to right of middle row of tufts might be edge of cluster of tufts?, object held by deity?

CONDITION   Surface in part worn and chipped; back break crisp; edges thin, worn; left face deteriorated. Salts on relief at right; no bitumen.

DIMENSIONS   GPW 0.075; GPH 0.08; GPTh 0.17 m

PUBLICATION   Canby 1998, p. 48, fig. 14 lower right

11 PART OF "ANGEL'S" DRESS

Register I, poor face?

Pl. 24

From storage

DESCRIPTION   Four undulating pleats and edge of fifth.

CONDITION   Surface worn with small pocks. Two droplets bitumen.

DIMENSIONS   GPW 0.04; GPH 0.07; GPTh 0.01 m

12 KING BEFORE GODDESS (GOOD FACE); BUTCHERS, CHARIOT, STANDARDS (POOR FACE)   U.3264 (main and corner fragments only)

12 good face, register II

Pls. 8a, 25, 26

12 poor face, register II

Pls. 7b–d, 27–30

Formerly register II, both faces

CONDITION   **12** good face: Three joining fragments. *Main block with king and goddesses.* Surface varies between excellent and worn with pocks, some large (as on poor face); layer with finished relief surface thinly flaked off in some areas; ear of goddess very worn; most of front of throne missing; tip of goddess's nose and fingers, tip of fingers of minor goddess, and king's buttocks worn off. Small drips of bitumen on relief face extending from top break; small deposits of salts on relief and on broken surface below.

Lower left corner with part of dais and throne, and part of register III. Worn join to main block; broken from core of stela along horizontal bedding plane running 0.02–0.08 m beneath relief surface;[8] surface preservation very good to very worn and chipped. Bitumen drips from bottom break into worn relief areas when upside down. Back reused as door-post socket (diam. 0.08 m; Pl. 7d); thick bitumen deposit on back break from above door-post socket into crack above join (i.e., deposited when corner fragment detached but in situ and face-down); some bitumen drips on adjacent main block and two specks of bitumen on upper edge of door-post socket but no salts pose question whether corner ever moved away from main block.[9]

Divider with part of throne on register I. Join along thin edge at base of divider; surface good except at right; all breaks old. Heavy salt deposit on back, drips over adjacent edges. Dais extended to right in plaster in 1927 and covered with plaster film.

12 poor face: Surface flaked, fractured into many thin fragments (Pl. 7b, c); very weathered breaks; some good surface on left side, part of relief at right worn beyond subject recognition. Numerous bitumen drips on reliefs and worn areas.

---

[7] Compare the goddess facing right, register II, good face (**12**; Pl. 25), where the tufts beneath the triangle get shorter from her hip to her knee.

[8] Note, the missing lower part of main block and the fragments of the right side of the stela on this face (**14**) detached along the same line of cleavage (Pls. 7d, 8a).

[9] See n. 13 below.

Pieces detached but found in place—face-up according to Legrain,[10] face-down according to Woolley.[11] Reliefs waxed, plastered, sawed off in field; saw marks now on surface of stone core behind three figures at left; saw mark on back of figure with goatskin; modern cut with smooth face (Pl. 8a) from behind right king's buttocks (**12** good face) to waist of figure leaning into bovine.[12] Before photography, pieces of butchering scene bedded in plaster then attached to other flakes or plaster-backing with shellac by Woolley at Ur (Pl. 7b); surface partly covered with mud mixed with water-soluble paint. According to drawing on shipping list, both scenes reconstructed onto slate background as separate segment before being shipped to Philadelphia: right section (standards) wrongly placed too low on register;[13] dismantled in 1927, placed correctly on core where joining surfaces still exist (Pl. 7c); in 1996, tips of seventh and eighth standards found in storage.

SAMPLING   1990, core sample 0.025 × 0.025 m, taken from broken surface of main block below attending goddesses on **12** good face; 1994, core hole resampled
FINDSPOT (U.3264, main and corner fragments[14])   *UE* VI, p. 97: "Filling of Lower Courtyard L.L." = "Dub-lal-mah"

DIMENSIONS   Entire block, GPTh 0.256 m. GPW good face, relief surface 0.984; GPH good face (main and corner fragments only) 0.57; GPW poor face, butchering scene 0.50; GPH poor face, butchering scene 0.34; GPW poor face, standards scene (main block only) 0.33; GPH poor face, standards scene 0.30 m. Weight of main and corner fragments combined, 218 kg
PUBLICATION   Good face: *AJ* V, pl. XLVIII, opp. p. 399; *UE* VI, pp. 75, 77, 97, pls. 41a, 42c, 43a, left (1925 reconstruction)

Poor face: Butchering scene: *AJ* V, pl. XLVII, 1 opp. p. 398 (as repaired in field); *MJ* 18, p. 87. Entire scene: *UE* VI, pp. 78, 97, pls. 41b, 44a (1925 reconstruction with **46** added. The drawing, *PKG* 14, fig. 38, p. 205 is based on this); Canby 1987, pp. 62, 63, fig. 7

13 CHARIOT WHEEL
Register II, poor face?

Pl. 30
From storage
DESCRIPTION   Section of chariot wheel appropriate size for missing chariot on **12** poor face; rounded knobs along outside of rim, double incised line along inside; something abuts last preserved knob.
CONDITION   Surface worn with some large chips; breaks worn with some globules salt. No bitumen.
DIMENSIONS   GPW 0.028; GPH 0.055; GPTh 0.02 m; Diam. of wheel 0.10 m
PUBLICATION   *UE* VI, pl. 43B.e

14 LOWER PART SEATED GOD (REGISTER I); KING BEFORE GOD (REGISTER II); GOD, KING, SERVANT (REGISTER III)   U.2761
Registers I–III, good face
Pls. 8b–d, 31–33
Formerly registers I–III, "obverse." Doweled together, restored with king before goddess, **12** good face, in exhibition in London (Pl. 3b);[15] separated from same before being shipped as one piece to Philadelphia, 1925; reassembled with **12** good face in Philadelphia, 1925–26;[16] dismantled and placed in reconstruction of whole stela, 1927.

Fragments labeled **a–f** by Woolley: **a**: dais, foot, register I plant tip, rod tip, register II; **b**: throne, dais, register I; crown, register II; **c**: skirt, register I; **d**: upper part throne, register I; **e**: hairdo of god, register II; **f**: lower part of king before seated god, register II; upper part servant, king, god, register III.
CONDITION   Six joining fragments, all fine-grained stone, most very well preserved; broken from stela along same cleavage plane as **12** good face; natural, straight-edged joins (Pl. 8b), tight at surface, less so beneath.

Right heel and most of left foot of figure seated on god's lap, register I, chipped off; face of god, register II, lost,[17] restored in plaster from cast of god on register III below (see Pl. 32); forehead, bridge, and tip of nose of king, cheek of servant, register III, damaged; latter has ridge-like area beyond eye. Back of **a**, **b** used as door-post sockets (Pl. 8c, d); striations from that use

---

[10] *MJ* 18, p. 89.

[11] *UE* VI, p. 78. Sawing them off in that position seems to me impossible.

[12] To lighten stone for lifting?

[13] Sketched in shipping list as shown in *UE* VI, pl. 44a without the right corner (catalogue no. **46**: feet and hoof); latter shipped separately according to the list.

[14] Corner fragment was probably located at a door, since it has a door-post socket.

[15] *UE* VI, pl. 43a.

[16] Seen in restoration in Coxe Wing, R. Dyson, "Archival Glimpses of the Ur Expedition in the Years 1920 to 1926," *Exp* 20 (1977), p. 21, fig. 25.

[17] For the original face of this god, see *AJ* V, pl. XLVII (= *MJ* 16, p. 48) (= *UE* VI, pl. 42d) (on Pl. 32 here); it may have been lost when making the cast at the British Museum that was mentioned in a letter, Kenyon to Gordon, 11/6/25, UPM Archives.

preserved, crisp on **a**. Salt deposits on both sockets, bitumen spots on **a**; numerous shallow, modern chisel marks back of **f**; bitumen drips from above sprinkled over the relief face, down into breaks (therefore when piece was face-up, already fractured); also onto back breaks of **a**, **c**, **e** (therefore when face-down, separated from stela); also on entire side of **e**, **f** near seated god, register II.

SAMPLING   1990, core sample 0.025 × 0.025 m, taken from area to right of dowel holes on back of **b**; 1994, core hole resampled

FINDSPOTS   **a**, **b**: used as door-post sockets in "impost boxes,"[18] probably in row of chambers along the wall northwest of the ziggurat;[19] *UE* VI, p. 96: **a**, **b** "from L4 PWD," **c** "from ES" = "Dub-lal-mah, building S of main court," probably "Room 17 of the E-Dub-lal-Mah";[20] *UE* VI, p. 96 gives no location for **d–f**; elsewhere (*UE* VI, p. 75), **d–f** described as from "gateway group," i.e., found inside or just inside doorway 33 of Dublalmakh court.

DIMENSIONS   Entire block, **14a–f**, GPW 0.718; GPH 1.05; GPTh 0.11 m

PUBLICATION   *AJ* V, p. 398, pl. XLVIII; *MJ* 16, pp. 49–55; *MJ* 18, pp. 83, 84, 86, 89; *UE* VI, pp. 75–78, pls. 41a, 42d, 43a (right); Canby 1987, p. 61, fig. 13 (lower register in reconstruction); Canby 1998, p. 46, fig. 12 (register I), p. 43, fig. 7 (register III)

15 POLE WITH STREAMER(?) AGAINST TOP OF BUILDING

"Register" III–IV, good face
Pl. 34
From storage

CONDITION   Three joining fragments of fine-grained stone, long separated, worn joins; middle, very worn, some chipping; small piece at left added in 1997. Salts on face of middle fragment; bitumen drip on right fragment; no salts or bitumen on back or side breaks.

DIMENSIONS   GPW 0.13; GPH 0.075; GPTh 0.02 m

PUBLICATION   (without left piece)   Canby 1993, p. 148, fig. 1; Canby 1998, p. 43, figs. 5, 7, p. 44, figs. 8, 9 top left

16 KNEELING FIGURE ABOVE BUILDING

"Register" III–IV, good face
Pl. 34
Part formerly "register" III–IV, "obverse"; knees, upper

arm from storage

CONDITION   Four joining pieces; fresh(?) breaks, thin edges; surface very good where preserved. Relief covered with bitumen; flows over right break; none on back.

FINDSPOT   *UE* VI, p. 97: "Filling of Lower Courtyard L.L." = "Dub-lal-mah"

DIMENSIONS   GPW 0.09; GPH 0.095; GPTh 0.012 m

PUBLICATION   *UE* VI, pl. 43d; Canby 1987, p. 61, fig. 13; Canby 1993, p. 148, fig. 1; Canby 1998, pp. 43–46, figs. 5, 7

17 TOE ABOVE LADDER

"Register" III–IV, good face
Pl. 34
Formerly "register" III–IV, "obverse," far left

CONDITION   Fine-grained surface; back break crisp. Covered with bitumen; goes over top right and left bottom break; in part scratched off; salt globules on crisp break at bottom of ladder.

DIMENSIONS   GPW 0.082; GPH 0.08; GPTh 0.035 m

PUBLICATION   *UE* VI, pl. 41a; Canby 1987, p. 61, fig. 13; Canby 1993, p. 148, fig. 1; Canby 1998, p. 43, fig. 7

18 FOOT ON BUILDING, ABOVE LADDER[21]   large part U.305

"Register" III–IV, good face
Pl. 35
Formerly "register" III–IV, "obverse"

CONDITION   Five joining fragments of fine-grained stone; back, bottom breaks crisp; surface well preserved. Sprinkling of bitumen drips on face over top right, left, part of bottom breaks.

FINDSPOT   *AJ* III, p. 324: "South-east entry court of the temple by the outer gateway"; U.305 (*UE* VI, p. 88): "T.T.B:4 [= "E-nun-mah"] with U.304"; U.304 (ibid.): "Found in the NW guard-chamber of the gateway from the Dublal-mah courtyard to the Sacred Way."

DIMENSIONS   GPW 0.15; GPH 0.24; GPTh 0.065 m. Thickness is 0.055 m less than that recorded at time of shipping, 1925

PUBLICATION   *AJ* III, pl. XXXIII (minus two joining fragments), p. 324; *MJ* 18, pp. 94, 95; *UE* VI, pp. 76, 88, pls. 41a, 43b; Canby 1987, p. 61, fig. 13; Canby 1993, p. 148, fig. 1; Canby 1998, pp. 42–43, figs. 5, 7

---

[18] See Chapter 1, n. 18.

[19] Not "SW," as in *UE* VI, p. 75: the original report, 1925, *AJ* V, p. 399, refers to room 5 on plan, ibid., p. 353, fig. 1,b, where there are no room numbers. In the final report on the ziggurat terrace in 1939, the impost-boxes are said to have been beside a doorway in the range of chambers along the northwest side rebuilt by Kurigalzu. "Range" describes the line of single rooms along the

wall better than room 5 in E Nannar, see *UE* V, p. 49 and *UE* VIII, plans 47, 48.

[20] Location given in *AJ* V, p. 399, quoted here Chap. 1, p. 2 (see plan ibid., p. 387).

[21] The piece was part of the University Museum's share of the finds, according to the division list of 3/21/23, UPM Archives.

19 BRICKS WITH SOMETHING ABOVE

"Register" III–IV, good face

Pl. 35

From storage

DESCRIPTION   Five courses of brick curve slightly outward at top; above top course, something raised almost to brick height, possibly a platform(?).

CONDITION   Well-preserved, fine-grained surface; all breaks crisp. No bitumen or salts.

FINDSPOT   *UE* VI, p. 97: "Courtyard filling L.L." = "Dub-lal-mah"

DIMENSIONS   GPW 0.05; GPH 0.09; GPTh 0.022 m

PUBLICATION   *UE* VI, pl. 43A.b (upside down); Canby 1998, p. 44, fig. 9 (upside down)

20 FOOT ON BRICKS

"Register" III–IV, good face

Pl. 35

Formerly "register" III–IV, "obverse," combined with leg on **47** and both given to servant behind king on **14f**

CONDITION   Fine-grained surface in good condition; break above ankle repaired before 1925–26 restoration. Drop of bitumen below ankle.

DIMENSIONS   GPW 0.05; GPH 0.076; GPTh 0.017 m

FINDSPOT   *UE* VI, p. 97: "Filling of Lower Courtyard L.L." = "Dub-lal-mah"

PUBLICATION   *UE* VI, pls. 41a, 43b; Canby 1987, p. 61, fig. 13; Canby 1993, p. 148, fig. 1; Canby 1998, pp. 42–43, figs. 5, 7

21 DOOR FRAME

"Register" IV, good face

Pl. 35

From storage

CONDITION   Two joining fragments; fine grained, well preserved; crisp breaks. Salt globules on face of right fragment; tiny drop bitumen on back.

DIMENSIONS   GPW 0.093; GPH 0.05; GPTh 0.04 m

PUBLICATION   Canby 1987, p. 61, fig. 13; Canby 1993, p. 148, fig. 1, pl. 12:4; Canby 1998, p. 43, fig. 7, p. 44, figs. 8, 9 top left

22 FOOT BESIDE BOTTOM OF LADDER

"Register" IV, V, and band, good face

Pl. 36

Formerly "register" IV, V, and band, "obverse"

CONDITION   Surface fine grained, well preserved; two slashes across foot on right; flat-edged breaks sides and bottom, as on **14**; extensive chisel marks lower part of back break.

DIMENSIONS   GPW 0.32; GPH 0.33; GPTh 0.08 m. Thickness is 0.035 m less than that recorded at time of shipping, 1925

FINDSPOT   *UE* VI, p. 97: "Filling of Lower Courtyard L.L." = "Dub-lal-mah"

PUBLICATION   *MJ* 18, p. 94; *UE* VI, pls. 41a, 43b; Canby 1987, p. 61, fig. 13; Canby 1993, p. 148, fig. 1; Canby 1998, pp. 42–43, figs. 5, 7

23 ARM OF BASKET CARRIER AND CHEST OF ANOTHER

"Register" IV, good face

Pl. 36

Formerly "register" IV, "obverse"

CONDITION   Two joining fragments; surface fine grained, worn, bodies badly chipped; breaks clean, worn. No salts or bitumen.

DIMENSIONS   GPW 0.10; GPH 0.11; GPTh 0.045 m

FINDSPOT   *UE* VI, p. 97: "Filling of Lower Courtyard L.L." = "Dub-lal-mah"

PUBLICATION   *MJ* 18, p. 94; *UE* VI, pls. 41a, 43b; Canby 1987, p. 61, fig. 13; Canby 1993, p. 148, fig. 1; Canby 1998, pp. 42–43, figs. 5, 7

24 BENT ARM IN FRONT OF BRICK BUILDING

"Register" IV, good face

Pl. 36

From storage

CONDITION   Old break joined with grayish glue, not removed; worn, fine-grained surface; no bitumen.

DIMENSIONS   GPW 0.06; GPH 0.035; GPTh 0.035 m

PUBLICATION   Canby 1987, p. 61, fig. 13; Canby 1993, p. 148, fig. 1; Canby 1998, p. 43, fig. 7, p. 44, fig. 9 bottom left

25 BASKET CARRIER BEFORE BRICK BUILDING

"Register" IV, good face

Pls. 9c, 37

Formerly "register" IV, "obverse"; small chip joining on left side from storage

CONDITION   Complete section of right side face preserved; latter roughly finished except along edge of relief; fine-grained stone in fair condition; figure damaged under arms; back worn with new chisel marks (Pl. 9c); the chipped back probably trimmed, 1927, to fit behind drummers, register IV, poor face (**28a**).[22] Thin

---

[22] It is a pity that the back of **25** was trimmed. This is the only place where the backs of good and poor face fragments may still have joined and confirmed the reconstruction of the stela. See Chapter 2, n. 6.

areas of salts on face; no bitumen.

FINDSPOT   *UE* VI, p. 97: "Filling of Lower Courtyard L.L." = "Dub-lal-mah"

DIMENSIONS   GPH 0.28; GPW 0.215; GPTh 0.09 m. Thickness is 0.025 m less than that recorded at time of shipping, 1925

PUBLICATION   *MJ* 18, p. 94; *UE* VI, pls. 41a, 43b; Canby 1987, p. 61, fig. 13; Canby 1993, p. 148, fig. 1; Canby 1998, pp. 42–43, figs. 5, 7

26   TWO COURSES OF BRICK

"Register" IV, good face? (not placed in reconstruction)

Pl. 37

From storage

CONDITION   Well preserved; surface flaked at top edge; all breaks crisp (fresh?). Thin salt film.

DIMENSIONS   GPW 0.105; GPH 0.05; GPTh 0.004 m

FINDSPOT   *UE* VI, p. 97: "Courtyard filling L.L." = "Dub-lal-mah"

PUBLICATION   *UE* VI, pl. 43A.a; Canby 1998, p. 44, fig. 9 top right

27   TWO COURSES OF BRICK

"Register" IV, good face? (not placed in reconstruction)

Pl. 37

From storage

CONDITION   Parts of four bricks on four small fragments, pre-1986 joins; fine-grained, well-preserved surface; bottom break crisp. One smear of salts on corner.

DIMENSIONS   GPW 0.06; GPH 0.025; GPTh 0.025 m

PUBLICATION   Canby 1998, p. 44, fig. 9 middle right

28A   SEATED KING AND "REFEREE" (REGISTER III); DRUMMERS (REGISTER IV); INSCRIPTION U.3265

Registers III–IV and band, poor face

Pls. 9a, 38–40

Formerly registers III–IV and band, "reverse"

DESCRIPTION   Joins fragment with inscription **28d**, also **28b** under relief surface:[23] the flat-edged break at bottom left joins flat break on **28b** (Pl. 9a).

CONDITION   Soft stone in poor condition, still full of salts; pocked, flaked, eroded; shattered or missing areas below relief surface impossible to fill; filling material absorbed by stone or too thick to flow. Thick bitumen drops into worn, pocked areas, over both sides

and top, bottom breaks; thick drops on back break; no bitumen drips on left side face of stela. Extensive modern chisel marks on back; large area chiseled-out across back below middle; consolidated in field before photography.

FINDSPOT   *UE* VI, p. 97: "Courtyard L.L." = "Dub-lal-mah"

DIMENSIONS   GPW 0.57; GPH 1.14; GPTh 0.18 m; weight 298 kg

PUBLICATION   *AJ* V, pl. XLVII, 1 (opp. p. 393) (earliest photograph, cropped); *MJ* 18, pp. 88, 90, 91, 92; *UE* VI, pp. 78–79, pls. 41b, 44c; inscription *UET* I, no. 44(b) fragment 1, p. 9, pls. H, III

28B   INSCRIPTION AND LIBATION   U.3328

Register V, poor face

Pls. 9a, 41

Formerly register V, "reverse"

CONDITION   Joins **28a**, under relief surface: a flat break at upper right joins a flat-edged break at bottom of **28a** (Pl. 9a). Little of surface preserved: dissolved, deeply pocked; pits, powdery at bottom, in left torso, skirt of king, bottom of altar, lower part libator's robe; here some thick shapeless fragments attached by Woolley, reattached by us; small, smooth areas ca. 0.01 m square on back = modern saw marks?; shallow modern chisel marks on damaged surface below libator, altar. Single bitumen drops on all surfaces except back, deposited while block face-up and already pocked and worn.

SAMPLING   1990, core sample 0.025 × 0.025 m, taken from middle top break; 1994, core hole resampled

FINDSPOT   *UE* VI, p. 97: "Filling of Lower Courtyard L.L." = "Dub-lal-mah"

DIMENSIONS   GPW 0.60; GPH 0.64; GPTh 0.19 m

PUBLICATION   *MJ* 18, pp. 88, 95; *UE* VI, pp. 79, 97, pls. 41b, 44c, bottom left

28C   INSCRIPTION FRAGMENT

Inscribed band above register V, poor face

Pl. 42

Formerly inscribed band above register V, "reverse"

CONDITION   Joins back of **28d** (Pl. 9b). Face not as worn and pocked as relief registers above; all breaks worn. Salt globules, left and back breaks, also covering entire flat bottom break.

SAMPLING   1990, core sample 0.025 × 0.025 m, taken from back break; 1994, core hole resampled

---

[23] The joins were unexpected. They occurred under the surface and were hidden by plaster. Woolley did not know of the joins, to judge from his remark that **28d** could be placed by means of the

inscription (*UE* VI, p. 79). Note also that the fragment is published as 3 in *UET* I, no. 44(b), pl. IX, whereas it actually joins between 1 and 2.

DIMENSIONS   GPW 0.31; GPH 0.30; GPTh 0.25 m.
PUBLICATION   *UET* I, no. 44(b) fragment 2, p. 9, pl. IX, no. 2; *MJ* 18, pp. 88, 90, 91; *UE* VI, p. 79, pls. 41b, 44c

28D FRAGMENT WITH INSCRIPTION AND TREE
Inscribed band and register V, poor face
Pls. 9b, 42
Formerly inscribed band and register V, "reverse"
CONDITION   Joins **28a** under latter's lower right edge; joins **28c** over latter's break on left side (Pl. 9b). Relief, most signs dissolved and pocked; surface of head lost. Bitumen drips from above on surface and top and left upper breaks; bitumen dripped on right break when fragment face-down; no salts.
DIMENSIONS   GPW 0.26; GPH 0.39; GPTh 0.17 m
PUBLICATION   *UET* I, no. 44(b) fragment 3, p. 9, pl. IX; *MJ* 18, pp. 88, 89, 91; *UE* VI p. 70, pls. 41b, 44c lower right

66A, B[24] SYMBOLS (ON STANDARDS?)   Right piece (**66b**) U.6587[25]
Pl. 52
66a: Left piece formerly register II, "reverse," above standards; middle piece from storage; **66b** (right piece): British Museum WA 118545 (1927-5-27-1)
CONDITION   Large pocks, pits, and worn breaks. Left piece modern chisel marks on back. Salts on top break of left piece; no bitumen. Top of right piece, doorsocket, diam. 0.08 m.
FINDSPOT   U.6587: *UE* VI, p. 98: "Lying on west side of courtyard of Dublal"
DIMENSIONS   **66a**: GPW 0.19; GPH 0.125; GPTh 0.075 m. **66b**: GPW 0.25; GPH 0.16; GPTh 0.30 m
PUBLICATION   Left piece: *UE* VI, pl. 41b, register II; right piece: description only, ibid. p. 98.

29 WRESTLERS AND ATTENDANT; NUDE SERVANT AND SEATED DEITY   U.18526
Register IV, poor face
Pl. 43
Formerly register IV, "reverse";[26] upper left corner of divider and liquid from storage
CONDITION   Part of surface smooth, fine grained; elsewhere worn, pitted, except for wrestler; back break worn almost flat; large pocks on dividers, dais, deity's skirt; some on background; shallow flaking above head of wrestler, below whisk; hollow under surface near diagonal crack. Much bitumen over relief surface; flowed over breaks at left, bottom, and over joining surface of top register at left; short drops over top break; flows from back onto right break; scratches on relief face from attempt to remove bitumen.
SAMPLING   1990, core sample 0.025 × 0.025 m, taken from top break above wrestler's head; 1994, core hole resampled
FINDSPOT   U.18526: *UE* VI, p. 103: "In the brick pavement of Kuri-Galzu's Ningal temple, front court." *UE* V, p. 55: In lower level of pavement, northeast edge of front court, Kurigalzu's Ningal temple, ziggurat terrace.
DIMENSIONS   GPW 0.59; GPH 0.57; GPTh 0.19 m
PUBLICATION   *University Museum Bulletin* (Philadelphia, 1933), p. 99, pl. V; *UE* VI, pp. 79, 103, pl. 44b; Canby 1987, p. 63, fig. 18; Canby 1998, p. 40, fig. 2

30 THIGH AND ARM OF WRESTLERS
Register IV, poor face?
Pl. 44
From storage
DESCRIPTION   Edge of lower right arm of figure pressed along edge of buttocks of different figure to right.
CONDITION   Surface dissolved and covered with tiny pocks; all breaks very worn. Bitumen on face, thick over the depression between arm and body; some tiny drips on back break.
DIMENSIONS   GPW 0.07; GPH 0.085; GPTh 0.015 m

31 PODIUM
Register IV, poor face, right?
Pl. 44
From storage
DESCRIPTION   Podium, same height as that in wrestling scene, **29**; ends short of side face; outline partly preserved.[27]

---

[24] This piece appears out of numerical order because **66b** was first examined by me on June 9, 1999, in the British Museum. Only then could I securely place it on the stela.

[25] The U. number shows that the piece was catalogued in the 1925–26 season, the year after the majority of the fragments were found. **66b** was found in 1996 in the British Museum Egyptian storage area, where it was left when the Assyrian and Egyptian antiquities were divided in 1957 (Julian Reade, pers. comm., Nov. 19, 1996). The fragment listed as U.6587 in *UE* VI, p. 98, is there described as:

"Upper portion of frieze shewing right tip of crescent, upper part of angel's headdress, and tip and flat end of star rays to left." Woolley's catalogue card in the British Museum reads differently: "Upper portion of frieze showing portion of crescent[,] upper part of headdress and two more crescents from left to right. Reused in later period as a door socket."

[26] There is no illustration of this piece in situ on the stela.

[27] The short podium, similar to that on **12** good face, register II, left, might suggest a goddess sat here.

CONDITION Surfaces grainy, worn with some large pocks; all breaks worn except for one small back break; bottom break dissolved. Bitumen on left of top break near relief face, bottom break, side face; salts on relief face and top and left breaks.

DIMENSIONS   GPW 0.135; GPH 0.115; GPTh 0.235 m

CHAPTER 5

Catalogue of Fragments Not Restored on the Stela

See pp. 29–30 in Chapter 4 for explanation of terms and conventions used in this catalogue.

32 TORSO AND LEFT BENT ARM OF WRESTLER(?)
Somewhere on register III or IV, poor face?
Pls. 12, 44
From storage
DESCRIPTION   Probably joined skirt, **33**.
CONDITION   Surface very worn with small to medium pocks overall; front of chest lost; breaks are dissolved. One tiny drip of bitumen on forearm; some salts in pocks on back break.
DIMENSIONS   GPW 0.07; GPH 0.07; GPTh 0.02 m

33 FRINGED SKIRT WITH TUFT OF WRESTLER(?)
Somewhere on register III or IV, poor face?
Pls. 12, 44
From storage
DESCRIPTION   Probably joined torso, **32**, at waist; too weathered to do so now.
CONDITION   Surface similar to that of **32**. Tiny drop of bitumen below tuft; no salts.
DIMENSIONS   GPW 0.06; GPH 0.075; GPTh 0.02 m

34 EDGE OF SKIRT AND LEG OF WRESTLER(?)
Somewhere on register III or IV, poor face?
Pls. 12, 44
From storage
DESCRIPTION   Slanted skirt over thick leg.
CONDITION   Entire surface worn with small pocks. No salts or bitumen.
DIMENSIONS   GPW 0.025; GPH 0.047; GPTh 0.01 m
PUBLICATION   *UE* VI, pl. 43B.h

35 KNOB
Somewhere on the top registers
Pl. 45
Formerly register I, "reverse," at top
DESCRIPTION   A gentle protuberance above the smooth background at the right side of **35** is what

Legrain took to be the remains of a crescent. The piece does not join the crescent block **6** or reach to the other face, as Legrain claimed.[1] A diagonal incised line along the left side marks the edge of the 1927 plaster over the ancient surface. The fragment preserves 0.13 m of the side face of the stela and that surface's convex curve is like the preserved part of **6** on the opposite, good face, proving it belongs on register I.
CONDITION   Worn; newly chipped area on back break.[2] Salt patches on face, right and left breaks; no bitumen.
DIMENSIONS   GPW 0.18; GPH 0.11; GPTh 0.12 m
PUBLICATION   Knob visible only in reconstruction: *UE* VI, pl. 41b

36 STAR POINT
Pl. 45
From storage
DESCRIPTION   The tip of a star point outlined inside has a narrower angle than does the star on **6**. Probably does not belong to stela.
CONDITION   Surface slightly worn; breaks worn. One bitumen drip on face.
DIMENSIONS   GPW 0.065; GPH 0.04; GPTh 0.105 m

37 LARGE-SCALE CROWN WITH CRESCENT
Somewhere on the top registers
Pl. 45
Formerly register I, "obverse"
DESCRIPTION   The crescent on the top of this four-horned crown identifies it as belonging to a moon god, probably Nanna, who was the tutelary deity of Ur. It is the only recognizable divine attribute on the stela. Unfortunately, the area below the horns preserves no part of the hairdo, which would indicate the gender of the deity and how he or she faced. We know that the crown did not belong to the seated god at the right on register I, good face, to whom it was given in the 1927 restoration, because one horn of the crown of that figure is preserved above the bun of hair on **2**.
CONDITION   Two joining fragments; surface mostly well preserved; all breaks worn. Small amount of salts

---

[1] "Tranche . . . s'éntendant d'une face à l'autre" in *RA* XXX, p. 114.

[2] Fresh chips of stone were found inside the stela during its dismantling, just below **1**, the "angel" block.

in crevice of lower horn; no bitumen.

DIMENSIONS   GPW 0.20; GPH 0.20; GPTh 0.03 m

PUBLICATION   *MJ* 18, p. 80, photo p. 82 left; *UE* VI, p. 76, pls. 41a, 45a

38 FRAGMENT FROM LARGE-SCALE DIVINE ROBE

Somewhere on the top registers

Pl. 45

From storage

DESCRIPTION   The left side of a figure in a tufted robe. The outside edge of a row of tufts and a small section beneath survives. A chip along the edge of the top tier makes the straight edge look wavy.

CONDITION   Worn overall; all breaks clean. No bitumen or salts.

DIMENSIONS   GPW 0.025; GPH 0.05; GPTh 0.005 m

PUBLICATION   *UE* VI, pl. 43B.f, upside down

39 FRAGMENT FROM LARGE-SCALE DIVINE ROBE

Somewhere on the top registers

Pl. 45

From storage

DESCRIPTION   The upper edge of a tufted robe hung over the bent lower arm of a deity comes from the left arm (the right arm is usually bare).

CONDITION   Stone dissolved overall. No bitumen or salts.

DIMENSIONS   GPW 0.04; GPH 0.03; GPTh 0.01 m

PUBLICATION   *UE* VI, pl. 43B.d, upside down

40 LARGE-SCALE HAND

Somewhere on the top registers

Pl. 46

Formerly register I, "obverse"

DESCRIPTION   A left hand has fingers outstretched. It comes from a figure facing right, hands upraised like the minor goddesses on register II, good face, or extended in greeting, like the seated goddess at left in the same scene. It could also come from a frontal figure.[3] The plump heel of the palm and profile of the thumb are carefully modeled.

CONDITION   Small pocks on surface; missing tips of all fingers except forefinger; breaks clean, evenly worn. No bitumen or salts.

DIMENSIONS   GPW 0.065; GPH 0.07; GPTh 0.025 m

PUBLICATION   Seen only in 1927 reconstruction: *UE* VI, pl. 41a

41 DIVINE CROWN

Pls. 12, 46

From storage

DESCRIPTION   A fragment with the back of the crown and hair bun of a male deity, facing left, is on the scale of the gods in registers II and III, good face. Traces of hatched lozenges on bun.

CONDITION   Fragile stone, worn, badly flaked at left edge, side; edges thin and sharp; back break crisp. No bitumen or salts

DIMENSIONS   GPW 0.041; GPH 0.07; GPTh 0.015 m

PUBLICATION   *UE* VI, pl. 43B.a, upside down

42 FRAGMENT OF DIVINE ROBE

Pls. 12, 46

From storage

DESCRIPTION   The bent tufts on this robe suggest it comes from the waist of a seated deity facing left. The division between the clusters of tufts is preserved, and the spacing between them suggests they belong to a deity on the scale of the gods on register II, good face.

CONDITION   Surface partly eroded; all breaks crisp. Droplets of salts on damaged relief surface; no bitumen.

DIMENSIONS   GPW 0.025; GPH 0.07; GPTh 0.015 m

43 FIGURE WITH AXE[4]

Pls. 12, 46

Formerly register V, "obverse"

DESCRIPTION   A figure, in a long robe that covers his bent left arm, faces left holding an implement with a rectangular blade upright in his left hand. He is approximately the size of the kings on register II, good face.

CONDITION   The relief is in good condition; broken areas on front face, worn. Drips on right break from

---

[3] Like a frontal goddess on Gudea stela: *BK* no. 48, Louvre.

[4] This fragment, **43**, and that of the bearded worshiper, **44**, are confused in Woolley's records. An illustration of **43** is on the list with other fragments for shipment in November 1925. The catalogue number U.6409 actually belongs to the bearded worshiper excavated in the 1925–26 season, i.e., **44**, *UE* VI, pl. 45e, since it matches the description in the Ur field catalogue and the Ur Photo Album no. 559, to which the catalogue refers. (A note attached to the photo there gives the erroneous number

U.6609.) The findspot given for U.6409 in *UE* VI, p. 98 is "KPS," which is between the Giparu and Ekhursag. This corresponds to the location given in the report to the Director, Nov. 25, 1925 (British Museum Archives), in which a photo of the bearded worshiper **44** is labeled "found in a wall of a later building second site," i.e., the site described in the report after the excavations of the Giparu, *AJ* VI, pp. 377ff.

However, ibid., p. 377, Woolley tells of a bearded figure from the stela in the destruction of the Giparu by Samsuiluna of the

puddle of bitumen on upper right corner; sanded to remove?; small drops of salts on bottom break. Short modern chisel marks and large chipped area on back break; cracked through shoulder since 1925 photograph.

DIMENSIONS GPW 0.19; GPH 0.23; GPTh 0.085 m. Thickness is 0.07 m less than that recorded at time of shipping, 1925.

PUBLICATION *MJ* 18, p. 96 right; *UE* VI, p. 79, pl. 44g, wrongly labeled U.6409

44 BEARDED WORSHIPER   U.6409[5]
Pls. 12, 47
Formerly register V, "reverse"

DESCRIPTION A bearded figure facing left has the edge of a hand preserved before his face. The angle of the proper left arm shows that it is extended. The head is the small size of the drummer on register IV, poor face. The hair style and beard is likewise similar to that drummer's and the wrestler's in the same register.

This is the only case on the stela in which someone with hair and a short beard wears the robe of the king and bald attendants. This recalls the statue of the crown prince of Lagash, Ur-Ningirsu, who is shown curly headed and bearded in contrast to his bald and clean-shaven father, Gudea.[6] Perhaps the hair and beard on the stela identifies the figure as crown prince.[7] One such bearded figure clothed in this robe appears on a floating fragment of the Gudea stelae.[8] Another is led before a seated goddess on a cylinder seal belonging to a scribe of Gudea.[9]

CONDITION Relief mostly very worn; bridge of nose, front of eye with brow preserved; back break worn, with fresh chisel marks. Bitumen drip on top of head, chipped shoulder, robe, bottom break; chip found in debris inside bottom of stela that joins top break. Traces of numerals visible on top of head: "A)...6...76[?]" possibly = "16676," the University Museum accession number for the whole stela.

FINDSPOT ?[10]

DIMENSIONS GPW 0.11; GPH 0.195; GPTh ca. 0.052 m

PUBLICATION *UE* VI, pls. 41b, 45e

45 FIGURE WITH CURVED OBJECT (WHISK?)
Pls. 12, 47
Formerly register III, "obverse"

DESCRIPTION A figure, bald and bare-chested, extends his muscular right arm across his chest. The figure is much smaller than others on the stela. In his left hand, raised to shoulder level, he grasps the handle of a badly denuded object that has a slight curve on the left side.[11] His inner ear is articulated only with a drill hole; his eyelid is heavier, eye rounder, and neck longer than those of other figures. No collar bone is indicated. The edges of the relief are cut back straight. If these peculiarities mean that the piece is from a different stela, it was one carved of the same stone as the other fragments.

CONDITION Surface mostly good; tip of nose, cheek damaged; bottom, left, and back breaks slightly dissolved. Many drops of salts on top break with thin film toward front face; small, thin bitumen patches on relief surface.

DIMENSIONS GPW 0.22; GPH 0.085; GPTh 0.055 m

PUBLICATION *MJ* 18, p. 96 left; *UE* VI, pp. 77–78, pls. 41a, 44d

46 FEET AND HOOF(?)
Pls. 12, 48
Formerly register II, "reverse," right, beneath standards

DESCRIPTION This fragment of an unusual scene is unfortunately in poor condition and difficult to interpret. On it, the feet and bare lower legs of a person facing left are placed far apart, perhaps to suggest motion. Behind him is what may be the foot of an animal. A human foot in this position would have the arch showing. This one is flat and there is a wide flange (or unfinished area) behind the heel. The leg is stretched forward at a 45-degree angle. A projection on the upper back of the leg looks like the beginning of an animal's underbelly but the surface here is too badly pre-

---

1st Dynasty of Babylon—a different and earlier context than the one just described but one that matches the context of U.6409 given on p. 44 in *UE* VI (with the erroneous reference to pl. 45b). The discovery of a piece of the stela in this destruction fill could be of importance for determining the date at which the monument was destroyed, see Chapter 1.

[5] This fragment is U.6409, illustrated *UE* VI, pl. 45e; see preceding note for confusion with **43**, the figure with an axe.

[6] *PKG* 14, pl. 64; Spycket 1981, no. 132.

[7] Spycket (ibid., p. 196) suggested that Ur-Ningirsu may have worn the beard because he was, as his eyes suggest, ill.

[8] *BK* no. 55, from Cros's excavations.

[9] Porada, *PM*, no. 274, pl. XLIII; inscription: ibid., text vol., p. 35. In commenting on the seal, Porada, noting the similarity to the Ur-Ningirsu figure, suggested the beard may be a survival of Akkadian traditions.

[10] See above n. 4 on problems with the provenances given for this piece.

[11] An implement like that on an inlay from Kish? See L. Watelin, S. Langdon, *Excavations at Kish IV–Oxford Field Museum Expedition* (Paris, 1934), p. 46, pl. XXX, 3.

served to rule out its being a skirt. Something with a vertical left edge preserved hangs down against the top of the foot. Part of the area above this is raised but no shape is discernable.

CONDITION   Crack behind figure's back leg; relief surface badly pocked, dissolved, in places soft; little original surface. Bitumen drops on surface and damaged areas; one drop on back; no salt deposits. The lower edge and right break of the divider was chiseled flat in antiquity (i.e., before the bitumen dripped), perhaps in an ancient repair.

DIMENSIONS   GPW 0.25; GPH 0.165; GPTh 0.035 m

PUBLICATION   *UE* VI, p. 78, n. 118 on p. 108, pls. 41b, register II right, 44a right

47 LEG AND SKIRT
Pls. 12, 49

Formerly, leg alone, on register III, "obverse"; restored together with foot on bricks, **20**, as left leg of servant behind king, register III, good face (**14**); skirt from storage

DESCRIPTION   A figure faces left, proper right leg probably raised. His skirt pulls taut over the thigh and up above the proper left knee. It is unusually short and has a very wide fringe that ends above the hem. The proper right kneecap is indicated by a groove, the left, by a raised area. The edge of the proper right calf appears along the left break.

CONDITION   Three pieces; excellent condition; leg more worn than skirt; breaks clean, worn. No salts; two bitumen drops on leg, left and back break.

FINDSPOT   "Filling of Lower Courtyard L.L." = "Dublal-mah"?[12]

DIMENSIONS   GPW 0.08; GPH 0.105; GPTh 0.02 m

PUBLICATION   *UE* VI, pl. 41a, register III, right; *UE* VI, pl. 43b, at right above building

48 SMALL LEG AND SKIRT
Pls. 12, 49
From storage

DESCRIPTION   Section across a small figure facing right, which includes both sides of the body, part of the diagonal skirt hem, and the sides of the proper left leg. This fragment must represent the part above the knee, as there is no curve for knee or calf. The surface of the skirt follows the shape of the underlying legs.

CONDITION   Surface and breaks in good but worn condition; leg surface lost. No salts or bitumen.

DIMENSIONS   GPW 0.065; GPH 0.048; GPTh 0.021 m

PUBLICATION   *UE* VI, pl. 43A.c

49 CROSSED ARMS
Pl. 49
From storage

DESCRIPTION   A lower right arm with clenched fist is crossed tightly over the lower left arm of another figure to the right, suggesting some sort of struggle. The crook of the arm of the figure at right is preserved. The arms belong to small figures approximately the size of the butchers on register II, poor face (**12**).

CONDITION   Worn overall; pocks, some large; back break dissolved. No bitumen; several tiny specks of salts.

DIMENSIONS   GPW 0.025; GPH 0.065; GPTh 0.012 m

PUBLICATION   *UE* VI, pl. 43B.j

50 LARGE HEAD
Pls. 12, 49

Formerly register IV, "reverse," right, on right side of restored drum in 1927 reconstruction; moved to left in same register when wrestlers (**29**) inserted

DESCRIPTION   The head of a large male figure facing left, with hair combed forward in thick wavy strands over the brow, would be approximately the size of the wrestler's on **29** if he had a beard. The curve in the worn jaw area suggests that he had no beard.

CONDITION   Surface very worn with small pocks; eye socket, back of eyelid, bridge of nose, lip-line visible in raking light; back break pocked and chipped. No salts or bitumen.

DIMENSIONS   GPW 0.07; GPH 0.08; GPTh 0.035 m

PUBLICATION   *MJ* 18, p. 90 top row center; *UE* VI, p. 79, pls. 41b, register IV, right, 45b

51 HEAD UNDER DIVIDER
Pls. 12, 49

Formerly register V, "obverse," left

DESCRIPTION   Facing right immediately under a divider is the head of a bearded male, approximately the size of the wrestler's on register IV, poor face (**29**). The figure must be standing on an unusual platform as high as that under the nude attendant in that scene. The hair is combed forward and the beard arranged in rows of curls. It is uncertain whether the thin lines in the moustache area are carved or are cracks from weathering like those on the nose. The proper left shoulder looks hunched.

CONDITION   Four tight-fitting fragments mended be-

---

[12] This findspot was given (*UE* VI, p. 92) for all brick fragments illustrated on ibid., pl. 43b, where **47** is illustrated.

fore first restoration of building scene; breaks worn except back; surface well preserved except for shallow chips in hair and beard. No salts; bitumen drop in eye partially scratched off.

Findspot "Filling of Lower Courtyard L.L." = "Dublal-mah"[13]

DIMENSIONS   GPW 0.07; GPH 0.14; GPTh 0.045
PUBLICATION   As single fragment: *MJ* 18, p. 94; *UE* VI, pls. 41a, 44e; in restored building scene: *UE* VI, pls. 41a, 43b

52 HEAD FRAGMENT
Pls. 12, 50
From storage
DESCRIPTION   The back of the head and rim of the ear of a figure facing right is probably the same size as the nude attendant in the wrestling scene on register IV, poor face (**29**).
CONDITION   Surface worn; back break dissolved. No salts or bitumen.
DIMENSIONS   GPW 0.028; GPH 0.04; GPTh 0.014 m

53 SMALL BEARDED HEAD
Pls. 12, 50
Formerly register IV, "reverse," right, on left side of restored drum in 1927 reconstruction; moved to left in same register when wrestlers (**29**) inserted
DESCRIPTION   The head of a bearded male facing right is about two-thirds the size of the wrestler's on **29**. His hair, combed forward from the crown, is clustered into an unusual style with groups of wavy strands. The short beard is covered with squares. The scale and style of the figure suggest it could come from a different monument.
CONDITION   Worn; crisp breaks; front of face lost; pock at throat; a bump on forehead. Some small specks of salts; no bitumen.
DIMENSIONS   GPW 0.045; GPH 0.07; GPTh 0.034 m
PUBLICATION   *MJ* 18, p. 90 top middle, *UE* VI, p. 79, pls. 41b, 45d

54 SHOULDER(?)
Pl. 50
From storage
DESCRIPTION   An finished relief edge in the shape of a proper right shoulder has a narrow width of background around it.
CONDITION   Relief surface lost; back break clean but

flaking. No salts or bitumen.
DIMENSIONS   GPW 0.04; GPH 0.045; GPTh 0.01 m

55 HAND(?)
Pl. 50
From storage
DESCRIPTION   Possibly a tapered lower arm and extended hand, in the scale of the king on register II, good face (**12**).
CONDITION   Surface partly lost; one edge of thumb(?), fingers(?) preserved; old breaks. Salt drop, bitumen on back.
DIMENSIONS   GPW 0.06; GPH 0.06; GPTh 0.02 m
PUBLICATION   *UE* VI, pl. 43A.f

56 OBJECTS ABOVE DIVIDER
Pl. 50
From storage
DESCRIPTION   Above(?) a base line there is, at left, an object shaped like a small foot (with something attached to the heel?); at right, a puzzling quasi-pyramidal element.
CONDITION   Relief surface lost; background well preserved. Two large globules of salts on bottom break; several drips and wide film on top break; no bitumen.
DIMENSIONS   GPW 0.24; GPH 0.06; GPTh 0.14 m

57 PART OF FIGURE IN FRINGED ROBE
Pls. 12, 51
From storage
DESCRIPTION   The complete cross section of the lower part of a figure is at the scale of the king on register II, good face, at left. A foot under the gown shows the figure was facing left and the central vertical fringe suggests the arm was bent over the waist. There is no sign of the flap over the arm, but the area the flap usually occupies is raised above the rest of the garment.
CONDITION   Good relief surface; center chipped off. No salts; thick bitumen from back break over onto left face and top and bottom breaks.
DIMENSIONS   GPW 0.12; GPH 0.085; GPTh 0.03 m

58 FRAGMENT OF FRINGED ROBE
Pls. 12, 51
From storage
DESCRIPTION   A portion of the right side of a figure in a fringed robe is preserved. The garment is unusual in having the wide border along the left edge of the ver-

---

[13] This findspot was given (*UE* VI, p. 92) for all brick fragments illustrated on ibid., pl. 43b, where **51** is illustrated.

tical fringe. The remains of the flap over the arm is also unusual in that it falls immediately beside the vertical fringe and has fine, thin fringes.

CONDITION   Relief surface worn; some medium size pocks; small shell imbedded left of fringe; back and bottom breaks dissolved. No salts or bitumen.

DIMENSIONS   GPW 0.065; GPH 0.055; GPTh 0.02 m

PUBLICATION   *UE* VI, pl. 43B.g, turned on left side

59 FRAGMENT OF FRINGED ROBE

Pls. 12, 51

From storage

DESCRIPTION   A section of vertical fringe raised above the left side of the garment has a narrow border on the right side. An incision to the right of the fringe marks the edge of the flap which is raised slightly. This could belong to the figure with an axe, **43** (Pl. 12).

CONDITION   Relief surface good. No salts; bitumen drips on relief and top break.

DIMENSIONS   GPW 0.03; GPH 0.015; GPTh 0.006 m

PUBLICATION   *UE* VI, pl. 43B.c, turned on left side

60 FRAGMENT OF FRINGED GOWN

Pl. 51

From storage

DESCRIPTION   One section of fringe exists on this fragment. The condition suggests it could come from **28a**.

CONDITION   Relief surface almost detached from very worn stone. No salts; two small drips of bitumen on broken surfaces beneath relief.

DIMENSIONS   GPW 0.04; GPH 0.07; GPTh 0.015 m

61 DRUMMER'S(?) SKIRT

Pls. 12, 51

From storage

DESCRIPTION   This small fragment has a section of a pleated garment like that worn by the drummers on register IV, poor face (**28a**).

CONDITION   Center surface worn off; all breaks old. Two globules of salts near bottom break; no bitumen.

DIMENSIONS   GPW 0.06; GPH 0.06; GPTh 0.02 m

62 DRUM FRAGMENT

Pls. 12, 51

From storage

DESCRIPTION   A small section of a drum rests on the top of a raised surface on which there is no trace of an inscription. The drum is of the same knobbed type as that on register IV, poor face (**28a**) but larger. **63** may belong to it. The only place the drum can fit on this face, assuming a drummer on either side, is on the right side of register V. There is no room for it in register III above the wrestling block, **29**. We might expect it there (i.e., in register III) by analogy to the drums shown side by side on Gudea stelae where there is sometimes only one drummer.[14] There is too much uncertainty to include the piece in the reconstruction.

CONDITION   Surface worn with pocks; back break dissolved; all breaks old. No bitumen or salts.

DIMENSIONS   GPW 0.09; GPH 0.11; GPTh 0.02 m

63 DRUM FRAGMENT

Pls. 12, 51

Formerly register IV, "reverse," right, restored drum in 1927 reconstruction; moved to register V when wrestlers (**29**) inserted in register IV.

DESCRIPTION   This fragment of a drum probably belonged with **62** and has been restored with it here (Pl. 12).

CONDITION   Surface and breaks very worn. Salt globules on top break; no bitumen.

DIMENSIONS   GPW 0.12; GPH 0.13; GPTh 0.04 m

PUBLICATION   *UE* VI, pl. 41b

64 GOATS(?)

Pls. 12, 52

From storage

DESCRIPTION   Part of two bearded goats(?) standing on a low platform facing each other. The platform is approximately the height of the top step of the goddess's dais on register II, good face (**12**). What appear to be a hoof, slender leg, beard, and edge of shoulder of the right goat are preserved together with the tip of the hoof and beard of the left. Both "beards" have slightly concave sides and are wide and cut off straight at the bottom. The legs are slenderer than those of the goat in the butchering scene on register II, poor face (**12**).

CONDITION   Worn surface with small pocks; large chip on platform and divider; back, left, top breaks slightly dissolved. Small globules of salts on back, left, top breaks; two tiny drops of bitumen on front.

DIMENSIONS   GPW 0.07; GPH 0.11; GPTh 0.03 m

---

[14] On *BK* no. 65 and Istanbul Archaeological Museum no. 5805, unpublished, the figure around the corner from the drum has arm raised, presumably to strike a drum. This suggests that two drums were used side by side. However, the fact that the second drum is always around the corner and that from certain angles, only one drum could be seen at a time could mean that the same drum is represented twice. See the drum without a drummer on *BK* no. 89. The relief around the corner is broken.

65 COW AND CALF
Pls. 12, 52
From storage
DESCRIPTION A bull calf stands in front of a larger bovine. Only the forward leg of the latter is preserved, and shows a raised disc at the knee joint.
CONDITION Surface slightly worn with small pits; old breaks except at lower left; shell in back break. No salts or bitumen.
DIMENSIONS GPW 0.07; GPH 0.06; GPTh 0.02 m
PUBLICATION *UE* VI, pl. 43A.e

66A, B
See following **28d** in Chapter 4, p. 37.

67 COILED ROPE(?)
Pl. 52
From storage
DESCRIPTION Section of curved object outlined by three rounded ridges that taper down to the background. These bend up just before the top break (as oriented here). A wide curved element extends in from right to cover a section of the lower ridges.
CONDITION Stone well preserved; crisp breaks. No salts or bitumen.
DIMENSIONS GPW 0.03; GPH 0.045; GPTh 0.02 m

68 CURVED OBJECTS
Pl. 52
From storage
DESCRIPTION On the end surface of a deep, narrow slice of the stela is a small section of three concentric ridges, the outside one the largest. These abut a thick element curved in the opposite direction.
CONDITION Surface well preserved; all breaks crisp but worn. Some salt globules on face and right break; three drops bitumen.
DIMENSIONS GPW 0.03; GPH 0.09; GPTh 0.10 m

69 POLE(?)
Pl. 52
From storage
DESCRIPTION A face along the left side of the stela has a vertical element with something else at right angles to it (as oriented here). To the right is a section of good surface. Above this is a raised area.
CONDITION Worn overall, front face covered with pocks; top, right and back breaks dissolved.
DIMENSIONS GPW 0.05; GPH 0.085; GPTh 0.02 m

70 WATER(?) ALONG PLATFORM
Pl. 53
Formerly register I, "obverse," before seated god
DESCRIPTION Two streams of liquid undulate along the front of a "platform" on top of a divider. Falling onto them, at the right side, a small element with two horizontal grooves remains. The left, sloping edge of this element is preserved; the right edge is broken.
CONDITION Relief surface mostly well preserved; small pocks; chips; breaks worn. No salts or bitumen.
DIMENSIONS GPW 0.105; GPH 0.105; GPTh 0.045 m
PUBLICATION *UE* VI, pl. 41a, register I, before the seated god

71 HEAPED BASKET(?)
Pl. 53
From storage
DESCRIPTION On the end of a deep slice through the stela is a triangular relief surface with a good edge. Midway down the left side (as oriented here) an edge of relief is preserved. There is also an edge of relief along the right side. Recessed above this is a ridge ending in a circular element at left. Above this are multiple wavy ridges, one surrounding an almond-shaped element. Something with surface lost projects to the right at the bottom of the preserved relief.
CONDITION All surfaces dissolved. Bitumen drip under salt deposit on back and upper right of break.
DIMENSIONS GPW 0.16; GPW carved surface 0.05; GPH 0.24; GPTh 0.20 m

72 MOLDING(?)
Pl. 53
From storage
DESCRIPTION What appears to be a section of an elaborate edge consists of a wide band that slopes inward (as oriented here), bordered at the top by two ridges, the outer lower than the inner. Something (that is now lost) projected at the bottom of the band.
CONDITION Surface fine grained; breaks dissolved. No salts or bitumen.
DIMENSIONS GPW 0.016; GPH 0.042; GPTh 0.035 m

73 CHARIOT FRONT
Pls. 12, 54, 55
From storage
DESCRIPTION A chariot front seen *en face* has a double curved handrail ending above the front. This has a midrib decorated with three vertical ridges. On either side of the midrib are two figures in horned crowns,

probably bullmen like those on the chariot fronts on the Gudea stelae.[15] A series of notches is visible on the proper right edge of the crown of the figure at left. It is just possible to make out the raised areas of the shoulders of both figures, and that of the face and beard of the one at the right. That figure's proper upper arm is preserved, as well as the lower edge of his proper right forearm, which crosses his waist. A vertical strut on the left side of the chariot front extends above it. Another strut projects from it to the left. This could be the arched pole or perhaps the pointed bottom of a quiver like those seen attached at an angle to the front of chariots in the Early Dynastic period.[16]

In the pocked area above the double curved handrail (the left tip of which is preserved) the battered outline of two rampant horned animals opposite each other, heads turned back over their shoulders, may be seen in a strong contrasting light. The outline of both pairs of horns and the lower part of the back legs of both animals, though damaged, may just be made out. The back side of the animal at left is completely missing. Judging from the short curved horns and the puff at the end of the tail of the right animal, these are bulls. Tendrils ending with a leaf may lie to the right of the right bull. A sketch of what, from the faint traces, I think was there is on Pl. 55.

CONDITION Four long-separated and worn but still joining pieces; soft, very poor surface, covered with deep pocks. No bitumen or salts.

DIMENSIONS GPW 0.13; GPH 0.19; GPTh 0.01 m

SAMPLING July 1991

74 OBJECT WITH CROSSED STRUTS(?)
Pl. 56
From storage

DESCRIPTION Under a raised area at the top of the fragment are clear but disjointed traces of some object or objects. One "strut" crosses over another at about a 40-degree angle. The upper end of the top strut (at left as viewed) abuts a wide area whose edges curve downward and seem to continue on the left side along the raised area on the small left piece. At the bottom of the fragment, the acute intersection of two other straight edges is preserved.

CONDITION Three fragments, the two large ones joined before 1986; surface mainly dissolved with wide,

deep pits; large pebble behind crossing elements. No salts; bitumen on lower right corner of relief face.

DIMENSIONS GPW 0.14; GPH 0.17; GPTh 0.03 m

75 "ANGEL" TORSO(?); ANIMAL HEAD(?)
Pl. 56
From storage

DESCRIPTION A large curved object is attached to something that is covered with wavy lines and has a double curved edge. In 1986 I thought this was part of a "flying angel" with a misshapen arm like the "angels" in the top registers. Turned differently (as here), the curved element looks like the horn of a very large animal with shaggy hair.

CONDITION Two pieces, joined before 1987; worn and chipped; incisions are clear. No salts; bitumen above "horn" partly scraped off.

DIMENSIONS GPW 0.075; GPH 0.05; GPTh 0.015 m

PUBLICATION *UE* VI, pl. 43A.g; Canby 1987, fig. 8, p. 59; Canby 1998, fig. 12

76 UNIDENTIFIED
Pl. 56
From storage

DESCRIPTION A worn fragment has several rounded and straight areas of no recognizable shape neatly raised above the background.

CONDITION All sides dissolved; grainy surface. No salts; numerous bitumen drips on the relief face; smaller ones on back break.

DIMENSIONS GPW 0.09; GPH 0.045; GPTh 0.015

77 CURVED ELEMENTS
Pl. 56
From storage

DESCRIPTION There are clear edges of two curved elements on the fragment, but surfaces are gone and the carved area too small to suggest the subject.

CONDITION Fine-grained stone; some areas well preserved; all breaks old. Small areas of salts on face; speck on left break; no bitumen.

DIMENSIONS GPW 0.03; GPH 0.92

78 FIGURE(?)
Pl. 56
From storage

---

[15] *BK* nos. 45a, 46a, b, 47 in Berlin, Paris, and Istanbul, respectively.

[16] Best represented in the Early Dynastic period by the series of chariots on the standard from Ur, Frankfort, *A and A*, pl. 36; for this and other examples, see M.-Th. Barrelet, "Peut-on remettre

en question la 'restitution materielle de la stele des vautours'?" *JNES* 29 (1970), p. 242, fig. 9 a, b, f, h (the last three quivers have pointed bottoms). For original of ibid., fig. 9 h see no. 255 in B. Buchanan, *Catalogue of Ancient Near Eastern Seals in the Ashmolean Museum, Cylinder Seals* (Oxford, 1966).

DESCRIPTION   The edges of the raised areas on this fragment suggest that a figure in a short skirt facing right may be represented. The surface is too damaged to be certain.

CONDITION   Condition similar to that of chariot (**73**): soft stone, dissolved, pitted, and pocked overall. Film of salts on the back; bitumen on lower left relief face.

DIMENSIONS   GPW 0.09; GPH 0.085; GPTh 0.03 m

79 STANDARDS(?)
Pl. 57
From storage

DESCRIPTION   Two upright poles(?) are discernable.

CONDITION   Condition similar to that of chariot (**73**); pits smaller; stone dissolved. Salt film on back; bitumen drop bottom of right pole.

DIMENSIONS   GPW 0.07; GPH 0.065; GPTh 0.015 m

80 STANDARDS(?)
Pl. 57
From storage

DESCRIPTION   Two upright poles and another element at right.

CONDITION   Two pieces with worn joins. Condition similar to that of chariot (**73**); pocks not as large. Salt film; no bitumen.

DIMENSIONS   GPW 0.09; GPH 0.09; GPTh 0.015 m

81 POLE(?)
Pl. 57
From storage

DESCRIPTION   Section of a rounded pole(?) at the left edge of the fragment.

CONDITION   Relief surface flaking; dissolved. Salts on front surface; no bitumen.

DIMENSIONS   GPW 0.045; GPH 0.06; GPTh 0.015 m

82 ELEMENT ABOVE DIVIDER
Pl. 57
From storage

DESCRIPTION   A small section of a divider below piece of the background and some relief at left on it.

CONDITION   Stone very fine grained; in part polished; breaks dissolved. Smear of salts on corner back break; small bitumen drip on top break.

DIMENSIONS   GPW 0.10; GPH 0.03; GPTh 0.07 m

83 ELEMENT ABOVE DIVIDER
Pl. 57
From storage

DESCRIPTION   Something (neither an undulating liquid nor a foot) lies along the outside edge above a divider. The top of the register below is preserved.

CONDITION   Surface good; old, clean breaks. No salts or bitumen.

DIMENSIONS   GPW 0.06; GPH 0.07; GPTh 0.035 m

84 CORNER FRAGMENT WITH POLE(?)
Pl. 57
From storage

DESCRIPTION   A deep slice of the edge of the stela preserves a small segment of two registers of the face. Along the left edge of the lower register is an upright pole(?).

CONDITION   Three very worn pieces; old breaks; relief surface more pocked than divider. Side face and part of front face covered with thick salts, in places over bitumen; large areas of bitumen on side and front faces, some in thick drops; right break clean.

DIMENSIONS   GPW side face 0.13; GPH side face 0.19; GPW front face 0.04 m

85 UNIDENTIFIED
Pl. 58
From storage

DESCRIPTION   A wide flat surface with non-parallel top and bottom edges is 0.05 m above the background. A convex edge is at the top of background.

CONDITION   Remaining surfaces well preserved; all breaks dissolved. Salts on top break; thick globules and film of salts on left break beside relief surface; scattered drops farther back; no bitumen.

DIMENSIONS   GPW 0.06; GPH 0.11; GPTh 0.105 m

86 EDGE
Pl. 58
From storage

DESCRIPTION   On the lower left corner of a fragment of background (as oriented here) is a rounded edge ca. 0.03 m high.

CONDITION   Fine-grained surface, smoothed; some chipped areas; all old breaks. Fat globule of salts on bottom break; fat, sagging globules on right and top break, salt film with salt specks on right edge of flat surface; no bitumen.

DIMENSIONS   GPW 0.17; GPH 0.06; GPTh 0.135 m

87 EDGE OF POLE(?)
Pl. 58
From storage

DESCRIPTION   A fragment of background with a small battered section of a rounded object at upper left (as oriented here).

CONDITION   Relief surface fine grained, smoothed; scattered small pocks; worn breaks clean. Sagging drop of bitumen on top break.

DIMENSIONS   GPW 0.06; GPH 0.11; GPTh 0.08 m

88 DIVIDER(?)
Pl. 58
From storage
DESCRIPTION   Part of a dividing band(?) projects an unusual 0.02 m at a sloping angle from the background.
CONDITION   Very fine grained stone; dissolved and weathered overall. No salts or bitumen.
DIMENSIONS   GPW 0.05; GPH 0.07; GPTh 0.035 m

89 INCISED SURFACE
Pl. 58
From storage
DESCRIPTION   One small edge of a raised flat surface is preserved in the upper left corner of the fragment (as oriented here); three faint incised lines at right are at an acute angle to this edge.
CONDITION   Stone weathered and chipped. Large globules salts on bottom, back, left sides; one drip on face; no bitumen.
DIMENSIONS   GPW 0.04; GPH 0.06; GPTh 0.025 m

90 EDGE
Pl. 58
From storage
DESCRIPTION   Raised edge at top left of background (as oriented here).
CONDITION   Relief surface with numerous wide, deep pocks, pink buff (rusty) tint overall; top break dissolved. Bottom break covered with salts; some on top, back breaks.
DIMENSIONS   GPW 0.09; GPH 0.06; GPTh 0.05 m

91 EDGES
Pl. 59
From storage
DESCRIPTION   Small raised areas remain at the top right corner and left edge (as oriented here) of a wide flat face.
CONDITION   Relief face smooth, mostly fine grained; small pebble in face; scattered pocks, some large. Heavy salt deposit on right and back breaks; some salts on face near right break; no bitumen.
DIMENSIONS   GPW 0.14; GPH 0.09; GPTh 0.06 m

92 DIVIDER
Pl. 59
From storage
DESCRIPTION   This section of a divider has a slightly tapered juncture with the background.
CONDITION   Very fine grained; relief surface smoothed; clean old breaks. No salts or bitumen.

DIMENSIONS   GPW 0.065; GPH 0.035; GPTh 0.015 m

93 DIVIDER
Pl. 59
From storage
DESCRIPTION   A section of a divider projects 0.01 m above the background.
CONDITION   Stone worn, pocked. No salts; bitumen drips in damaged areas on face.
DIMENSIONS   GPW 0.05; GPH 0.085; GPTh 0.05 m

94 CORNER
Pl. 59
From storage
DESCRIPTION   This section of a corner comes from a background area.
CONDITION   Fine-grained, smooth surface, well preserved; clean breaks. Speck of salts front face and back break; no bitumen.
DIMENSIONS   GPW 0.04; GPH 0.065; GPTh 0.035 m

95 SURFACE
Not illustrated
From storage
DESCRIPTION   Deep, diagonal sliver through stela with one small recessed worked surface.
CONDITION   Dissolved and pocked overall. Scattered thick salt clusters on bottom (as oriented here) break; also on right break with mildew(?); bitumen left of worked surface; large drip on bottom break.
DIMENSIONS   GPW 0.23; GPH 0.08; GPTh 0.27 m

96 BACKGROUND
Pl. 59
From storage
DESCRIPTION   Deep slice through stela with one plain worked face.
CONDITION   Smooth surface; some scattered pocks, several large; large globules salts on top, bottom breaks; thin salt skin running over left break; salts with some bitumen(?) on top of back break.
DIMENSIONS   GPW 0.15; GPH 0.07; GPTh 0.25 m

97 BACKGROUND
Pl. 59
From storage
DESCRIPTION   Small section of stela probably containing background.
CONDITION   Stone fine grained with scattered small pocks; right side dissolved with larger pocks. Large globule salts left upper corner; several on left break; some salts on top, bottom breaks; no bitumen.
DIMENSIONS   GPW 0.13; GPH 0.06; GPTh 0.062 m

APPENDIX 1

The Text of the "Ur-Namma" Stela

Steve Tinney

The text of the stela[1] was published in copy as *UET* I, 44(a) and (b), with a photograph of fragment 1 of part (b) on pl. H. It is republished here in line drawing and tonal copy (Pl. 60). Although the copy in *UET* I sometimes presents as perfectly clear signs that can be read only partially and with great difficulty, the photograph in *UET* I suggests that the inscription itself has not deteriorated dramatically over the last seventy years. Some specific points of disagreement or difficulty are addressed in the commentary below. Other recent scholarly editions of the stela inscription are to be found in Steible, *FAOS* 9/2, 134–138 (as Urnammu 29), and Frayne, *RIME* 3/2, 57–58 (as Ur-Nammu

E3/2.1.1.22).

The following edition of the inscription omits the piece *UET* I, 44(a), Ur-Namma's name, which has now been shown not to be part of the stela (see Chapter 1, n. 3). The old reconstruction of the monument shows that *UET* I, 44(b) fragments 1, 2, and 3 join in the order 2+3+1. The transliteration given below is based on renewed collations, but the surface of the monument is so pitted and difficult to read in places that it is unlikely that any reading of the text could be considered completely definitive.

Note: signs underlined are given on the hand copy in *UET* I, but are not legible on the stela.

TEXT AND TRANSLATION

Column i

(approximately 32 lines missing)

1'.	[...]	...
2'.	[...] ʳxʼ	...
3'.	[...] IM	...
4'.	[...] ʳxʼ [...]	...

(gap of approximately 2 lines)

0".	[íd...]	the canal "..."
1".	ʳmuʼ-[ba-al]	he dug;
2".	íd[...]	the canal "...
3".	[...]	..."
4".	ʳmuʼ-ba-a[l]	he dug;
5".	íd [x-(x)]-na	the canal "...,"
6".	ʳíd? (x) xʼ DU?	the canal? "...
7".	ᵈnanna	(of?) Nanna,"

8".	mu-ba-al	he dug;
9".	íd ᵈʳnannaʼ-/gú-gal	the canal "Nanna-gugal,"
10".	ʳíd ki-sur-raʼ	the boundary-canal
11".	[ᵈ]ʳnin-gírʼ-su	of Ningirsu,
12".	ʳmuʼ-ba-al	he dug;
13".	íd gú-bi-eridu/ᵏⁱ-ga	the canal "Gubi-Eriduga,"
14".	íd ʳÍL?ʼ-[x]	the canal...
15".	ᵈnin-ʳgír-suʼ	of Ningirsu,
16".	mu-ba-a[l]	he dug.

Column ii

(approximately 27 lines missing)

1'.	[...] ʳKIʼ	...

---

[1] The following bibliographic abbreviations are used in this Appendix:

ASJ = *Acta Sumerologica Japan*

Steible, *FAOS* 9/2 = H. Steible, *Freiburger altorientalische Studien* 9/2: *Die neusumerischen Bau- und Weihinschriften*, Teil 2. Stuttgart: Franz Steiner, 1991.

PSD B = *Pennsylvania Sumerian Dictionary*, B. Åke W. Sjöberg, ed. Philadelphia: University Museum, 1984.

Frayne, *RIME* 3/2 = D. R. Frayne, *Royal Inscriptions of Mesopotamia, Early Periods* 3/2: *Ur III Period (2112–2004 B.C.).* Toronto: Univer-

sity of Toronto Press, 1997.

UET I = C. J. Gadd and L. Legrain, *Royal Inscriptions. Ur Excavations*, 2 vols. Vol. I: *Texts.* London: Joint Expedition of the British Museum and the Museum of the University of Pennsylvania to Mesopotamia, 1928.

Royal inscriptions of Ur-Namma are cited according to the numbering in Steible, *FAOS* 9/2, with the numbers used in Frayne, *RIME* 3/2 following in square brackets. Year names of the Lagaš and Ur III kings are cited according to the lists given in pp. 317–329 of M. Sigrist and T. Gomi, *The Comprehensive Catalogue of Published Ur III Tablets* (Bethesda, MD: CDL Press, 1991).

2'.	[x(x)]-ˈxˈ-šè	…
3'.	[x]-ˈxˈ-da	…
4'.	[x] mu-da-gi₄	…
5'.	lú ˈáˈ- níg/-hul-d[ím-ma]	whoever gives a malicious instruction
6'.	[íb-ši-ág-/gá-a]	toward it (the stela),
7'.	[lú mu-sar-ra]-ba	erases its inscription,
8'.	[šu bí]-íb-/[ùr-a]	

(approximately 3 lines missing)

| 1". | ˈxˈ [x(x)]/[x(x)] | … |
| 2". | ˈxˈ [x(x)] ˈxˈ-ga | … |

3".	lu[gal? x(x)] GI/ZI?	king of …
4".	[…]	…
5".	luga[l…]	king of …
6".	ˈxˈ […]	…
7".	lugal […]	
8".	ˈdˈ […]	(the god) …
9".	nin ˈxˈ [x(x)]/ˈxxˈ [x(x)] AN	queen of …
10".	nam [x(x)] ˈxˈ	may they curse (that person).
11".	ˈxˈ-[…ku₅]	

(approximately 4 uninscribed lines to end of column)

EPIGRAPHIC NOTES

i 6". *UET* I's MAḪ is quite uncertain, and the extant traces have exactly the form of **DU** in monumental script. Perhaps read ˈSUḪUŠˈ.

i 14". This line was read and copied **íd gú-úr** in *UET* I, but neither **GÚ** nor **ÚR** is convincing in the present state of the inscription, which most closely resembles the beginning of **ÍL**.

ii 5'. Previous editors of the text have corrected *UET* I's **DA** to **Á**. Collation shows that there are traces of small inscribed wedges indicating that **Á** was on the original.

ii 9"ff. The curse element restored in 7'–8' often continues with **mu-ni bí-íb-sar-re-a**, "and inscribes his name," which might have occurred following 8', split over 2 or 3 cases. However, note that Ur-Namma 40 has an abbreviated form of this curse element which omits the second clause.

ii 11"ff. At the end of column ii of the inscription is a level area on which traces of erased case rulings are just identifiable. Presumably the cases were engraved first therefore and some were left unused at the end of the text and so erased. The traces indicate that at least 4 lines were left blank at the end of column ii.

RECONSTRUCTION OF THE INSCRIPTION

The even spacing of the cases and the reconstruction of the true breadth of the stele allow the inference that about 32 cases are missing from the start of column i. Of this, one can reasonably estimate, based on extant Ur-Namma inscriptions, that as much as half may have been the normal preamble of dedicatory and titulary material, meaning that about 16 short lines of substantial content may have been lost.

The end of the text is clearly a curse formula, of which ii 5' is probably the first line. The formula is too fragmentary to permit a complete reconstruction, but the typology of such formulae is well known, and the element given in ii 5'–6' is normally the first element of the curse formula.[2]

WHOSE INSCRIPTION?

Since geological testing has left the stele without certain attribution, it is worth reviewing the evidence that might bear upon this issue. Two angles of approach are offered by the language of the inscription and the names of the canals.

---

[2] For a useful description, see P. Michalowski and C. B. F. Walker, "A New Sumerian Law Code," Pp. 383–396 in *DUMU E₂-DUB-BA-A: Studies in Honor of Åke W. Sjöberg*, ed. H. Behrens, H. D. Lod- ing, and M. Roth (Occasional Publications of the Babylonian Fund 11, 1989).

LANGUAGE

The verb used for canal-digging, **ba-al**, exhibits certain distributional features. As observed by H. Steible, *FAOS* 9/2, 117, **ba-al** is not used in the Old Sumerian royal inscriptions when canal-digging is referred to. Although Ur-Namma is the only king of the Ur dynasty to use the term **ba-al** in his inscriptions, the expression occurs in several Lagaš year names,[3] and is relatively common in year names and in Old Babylonian inscriptions from Isin, Larsa, and Babylon.[4]

From the late third millennium onwards, **ba-al** was evidently the standard verb for "not only the initial digging of a water course but also its subsequent enlarging or deepening"[5] and one cannot therefore attribute the stele to Ur-Namma on this basis alone. It is a striking fact, however, that until Lipit-Eštar of Isin the only royal inscriptions proper describing canal-digging with the verb **ba-al** are those of Ur-Namma, for whom four such accounts are known.[6]

CANAL NAMES

Only two canal names can be deciphered on the stele inscription: Nanna-gugal and Gubi-Eriduga. The Gubi-Eriduga canal, which is not known from elsewhere, cannot be localized.[7]

The Nanna-gugal canal is well known from several contexts, the most leading of which is an Ur-Namma inscription recording its construction: **íd-da ᵈnanna-gú-gal mu-bi íd ki-sur-ra-kam mu-ba-al** "he built the canal whose name is Nanna-gugal, this is a boundary canal."[8] This canal is known from administrative texts dating from the Ur III to the Kassite periods, and also appears in lexical texts.[9]

CONCLUSIONS

It is presently impossible to attribute the stele with complete certainty on the basis of the inscription. As it is impossible that the Nanna-gugal canal could have been used from Ur III to Kassite times without periodic maintenance work, the fact that Ur-Namma is the only king for whom we have extant data attesting to work on the canal is not sufficient to assign the stele to that ruler.

While the philological information from the stele makes attribution to Ur-Namma plausible, therefore, it does not independently confirm this.

---

[3] Gudea Year Name 2: **mu íd ᵈnin-gír-su-ušumgal ba-ba-al-la**, Gudea Year Name 17: **mu-íd ᵈpirig-gin₇-du ba-ba-al-la**; Urbaba Year Name b: **mu íd giš-šub-ba ba-ba-al-la**. Year names are cited from the collation of M. Sigrist and P. Damerow at http://mpiwg-berlin.mpg.de/Yearnames.

[4] See *PSD* B 10–12.

[5] M. Civil, *The Farmer's Instructions* (Aula Orientalis Supplementa 5) 109.

[6] Ur-Namma 22 [E3/2.1.1.39], 23 [E3/2.1.1.26], 24 [E3/2.1.1.40], 28 [E3/2.1.1.28].

[7] F. Carroué, "Etudes de Géographie et de Topographie Suméri-ennes: III. L'Iturungal et le Sud Sumérien," *ASJ* 15, 11–69, esp. 44.

[8] Ur-Namma 28 i 10–13, Steible, *FAOS* 9/2, 131; Frayne, *RIME* 3/2, 64.

[9] See most recently, F. Carroué, *ASJ* 15, 45 and n. 183. Carroué also briefly discusses the various still-inconclusive suggestions for identifying the canal.

Conservation of the "Ur-Nammu" Stela

Tamsen Fuller

GENERAL CONSTRUCTION

Because of the paucity of records, almost all the information concerning the reconstruction of the stela was gained during the actual process of removing the limestone fragments from the restoration materials that formed the larger part of the reconstructed stela. For example, only during the final stages of the dismantling was it realized that the stela had been reconstructed in situ in the gallery of the museum.

Basic construction techniques and materials were consistent with the times: wood, iron rod and wire, wire mesh, plaster, and paint. The stela had been built from the floor up, based on tie rods bolted into the floor and a foundation of plaster and bricks (Pl. 9d). Wood framing had been used to provide "floors" for various parts of the upper registers. Much of the stela was actually hollow.

Large blocks had been positioned with the aid of metal rods sometimes doweled directly into the stone, wood braces, and quantities of plaster, sometimes reinforced with flat iron bars. Unfortunate liberties had been taken with some of the pieces, which were trimmed with chisels to fit the space available (Pl. 9c). Many of the uncarved fragments thus removed were found in surrounding plaster or inside the stela at the bottom.

Expanses of flat background had been fashioned with flat wood pieces or, more usually, wire mesh supporting a plaster facing. Smaller pieces of the original relief had been inserted into pockets in the plaster, often backed with wire mesh. The restoration plaster had been painted, apparently at two times in the stela's history. The later color was a gray-green.

Other materials that had been used on the stone of the stela included various coatings and adhesives, colored filling plasters, and overpaint from the painting of the surrounding plaster. Some of these materials are likely to have been applied in the field at Ur, or in previous restorations. The coating that had been most commonly rubbed over relief surfaces appeared to be a wax, colored with either pigment or soil. The common adhesive was shellac (Pl. 7b).

GENERAL TREATMENT

The stela was treated in a series of steps, beginning with dismantling the reconstruction and removing the stone pieces, and taking them to another space for additional examination and cleaning. The stela was taken apart from the top. First the perimeters of the stone blocks were exposed by removing surrounding plaster with percussive techniques, mostly using hammers and chisels. Small pieces were lifted out by hand on their backing plaster, while larger pieces, some weighing several hundred pounds, were lifted down with heavier equipment. These larger pieces were padded with polyethylene foam, secured with padded steel cable, and lifted out and down to waiting wheeled dollies with a winch-like "Come-Along" hanging from the apex of a large aluminum tripod.

Once in the conservation room, restoration materials were removed from the limestone fragments. The purpose in cleaning was to reveal original stone surfaces clearly enough that researchers could study the fragments.

Again, percussive techniques were used to remove the majority of the plaster from the stone, while organic solvents were used to remove overpaint and old adhesives. Metal dowels were removed, sometimes by loosening them from the plaster filling the dowel hole and pulling them out, and sometimes by drilling the metal out.

Final cleaning was conducted using aqueous methods, which were purposely delayed until this point because of the salty nature of the limestone. Some of the smaller pieces were immersed in water and brushed to loosen burial soil, plaster dust, and the waxy mud-colored coatings simulating "mud." Larger blocks that could not be immersed safely were brushed with water on soft brushes and the soiled water vacuumed away. Plaster in stone pores was moistened and removed with scalpels and steel needles.

The stela has not been reconstructed, although some small fragments were joined using a stable and reversible acrylic resin.

As treatment of the stela proceeded, the extent to which it had been restored and the original pieces altered became increasingly clear. The limestone itself was often found to be in poorer condition than had been originally thought. These factors meant the treatment project took longer and was more difficult than envisioned.

TREATMENT OF THE BUTCHERING SCENE

The butchering scene (**12** poor face, left; Pl. 29), in particular, had been heavily restored, so that it was impossible to distinguish original stone from restored features. The scene was at points almost paper-thin, in contrast to the thick block of the king before goddess (**12** good face; Pl. 25) to which it had been adhered with plaster and shellac. Because of the thin and fragmentary nature of the scene, its removal from the backing plaster was dangerous, difficult, and time consuming.

Sections along with their backing plaster were removed from the parent block using small chisels and saws. Once the plaster-embedded scene was removed, the plaster was wetted with water and mechanically scraped and picked from the back of the relief. The stone proved to be laminated, and splintered pieces had been attached to each other and to the surrounding plaster with layers of shellac mixed with plaster (Pl. 7b). To remove this combined material, some sections were immersed in solvent combinations. Immersion in fluids rendered the stone even more fragile and further prolonged treatment time.

The butchering scene was reconstructed using a minimum of adhesive, reinforcing backing material, and glass bead filler. Although in some places it securely joins the back of the king before goddess scene on **12** good face (Pl. 7c), for safety's sake it remains a separate work at present.

APPENDIX 3

Fragments From Other Monuments

The following pieces are published here because they were either restored on the stela in 1927 or found among the fragments labeled "Ur-Nammu stela" in storage in the University of Pennsylvania Museum.

In 1991, specimens for mineralogical examination were taken from all fragments whose appearance suggests they do not belong to the stela, except for **A1**. These were given to Dr. Robert Giegengack, Department of Earth and Environmental Science, University of Pennsylvania. Final results are not available except for **D1**, fragment of Ur-Nammu skirt (see n. 4 below).

See pp. 29–30 in Chapter 4 for explanation of terms and conventions used in this catalogue. The University of Pennsylvania accession numbers follow the identification.

A1 HEAD OF GOD (98-9-12)
Pl. 61
From storage
DESCRIPTION Stone gray, lightweight, porous, with fine grains like **A2**. A god facing left has wavy hair pulled back across the forehead beneath the crown and swooped up along the edge of a back horn to at least where the horn turns inward. This arrangement has no parallels on the stela. Part of the profile, the heavy lids at the front of the eye, and the outline of the ear are still visible.
CONDITION Orange tinge to relief surface; very worn, chipped; all breaks old; left break flat (natural?). Clusters of salts on back break; no bitumen.
DIMENSIONS GPW 0.08; GPH 0.075; GPTh 0.03 m
PUBLICATION Reconstructed as head of "angel" in Canby 1987, p. 59, fig. 8; Canby 1998, p. 46, fig. 12

A2 LYRE (98-9-13)
Pl. 61
From storage
DESCRIPTION Gray, light, porous, grainy stone like **A1**. The lyre has seven thick strings that splay out slightly toward the top. To the right of the strings is a section of a wide frame. The tops of the five strings to the left of the frame are preserved. The third from right is shorter than the first two. The fourth from right is longer. The fifth and sixth strings are probably also longer but the damaged tops make this uncertain. The seventh string from the right looks splayed out. The length of the strings suggests the top piece must have been concave[1] or possibly that the arm of the player rested across the strings. At the left edge, a short straight element could be part of an animal incorporated into the frame, similar to the bull's head on a lyre of a Gudea stela fragment and the well-known lyres from the Early Dynastic period.[2]
CONDITION Some orange-buff areas not associated with relief; very pitted, pocked, and worn; all old breaks. Salt film(?) on some dissolved areas; no bitumen.
DIMENSIONS GPW 0.095; GPH 0.08; GPTh 0.043 m

B1 OBJECT (98-9-15)
Pl. 61
From storage
DESCRIPTION Dense, gray stone like **B2**, **B3**. The outlines of this object are for the most part clear but I cannot identify it. Left (as oriented) of a frame with tapered edge lies a cymbal-like object with an articulated knob on top. The curved profile of the left edge may be due to a chip. There is something below the "cymbal."
CONDITION Surface worn with some chipping; all old breaks; chipped areas on back, bottom breaks; some sparkle. Spots of salt film on relief surface; one spot bitumen(?) on face.
DIMENSIONS GPW 0.13; GPH 0.05; GPH 0.065 m

B2 ROPE AND BOARDS(?) (98-9-14)
Pl. 62
From storage
DESCRIPTION Heavy, dense, gray stone like **B1**, **B3**. Three flat planks lie above (as oriented here) a log with rope wound tightly around it at an angle. The broken area to the right of the rope has puzzling

---

[1] Like the famous lyre on a stela fragment from Tello, *BK* no. 90a, which D. Collon, "Leier Archäologisch," *Reallexikon der Assyriologie* VI, fasicule 7–8 (1983), p. 570, classified as "type II, Asymmetrical, no. 1, example j." The Tello example's cross piece is, however, slightly curved, as is the left side of the sound box.

[2] For Gudea stela lyre, see preceding note; actual example from the Ur royal tombs, *Treasures from the Royal Tombs of Ur*, eds. R. L. Zettler and L. Horne (Philadelphia: University of Pennsylvania Museum, 1998), pp. 53–57.

straight incisions.

CONDITION Crisp carving; smooth relief surface; all old breaks; back break fractured and chipped. Salts on top break; no bitumen.

DIMENSIONS GPW 0.12; GPH 0.05; GPTh 0.11 m

B3 BARGE(?) (98-9-16)
Pl. 62
From storage
DESCRIPTION Dense, heavy gray stone with fine grains like **B1**, **B2**. Four "logs" over a longer one could represent a barge.[3] The small logs have a slightly curved surface, that of the long one is fully rounded.
CONDITION Well preserved; all breaks worn. Patches of yellow-buff film on relief surface, back break; no bitumen.
DIMENSIONS GPW 0.08; GPH 0.05; GPTh 0.04 m

C1 POLE (98-9-17)
Pl. 62
From storage
DESCRIPTION Dense, light-colored, flint-like stone like **C2**. A pole with finely grooved surface is preserved.
CONDITION Three joining pieces; pre-1986 mends; polished white film on relief surface; scattered iron stains; some breaks fresh(?). Salts on back break; bitumen drips on face.
DIMENSIONS GPW 0.055; GPH 0.06; GPTh 0.03 m

C2 CORNER(?) (98-9-18)
Pl. 62
From storage
DESCRIPTION Stone like **C1**. A sharp corner is raised above a flat surface.
CONDITION All breaks except bottom old. Some white salts on back; no bitumen.
DIMENSIONS GPW 0.03; GPH 0.03; GPTh 0.012 m

D1 SKIRT WITH INSCRIPTION OF UR-NAMMU (98-9-19)   U.3215
Pl. 63
Formerly (1925) register I, "obverse," on reconstructed king's skirt; in 1927 reconstruction, moved to register III, "obverse"; small piece at lower right from storage
DESCRIPTION Grayish pink stone with red specks.[4] The important fragment with a section of a fringed robe bearing the inscription "Ur-Nammu King of Ur" joins a small piece from storage. The latter has the fringe of the flap restored in plaster on the stela in 1927. Like the vertical fringe on the robe, it is finer and longer than that on garments on the stela. The new fragment also has the missing right edge of the figure, who was larger than the kings of the stela. The vertical incised fringe at left (as viewed) has no border. The vertical fringe at right side, which is raised, has a border on the left side. The area where the flap is usually seen is merely raised.
CONDITION Four joining pieces; old worn break at lower right; face in good condition; back breaks dissolved. Salt speck on the face of the small piece;[5] bitumen drops on the face across the inscription.
FINDSPOT *UE* VI, p. 96: "Courtyard in front of Dublal"
DIMENSIONS GPW 0.14; GPH 0.18; GPTh 0.02 m
PUBLICATION *AJ* V, opp. p. 399, pl. XLVIII; *UET* I, no. 44(a), p. 9, pl. VII; *MJ* 18, p. 85 = *UE* VI, pl. 43a (first reconstruction), pl. 41a (1927 restoration), register III, p. 96; Canby 1987, p. 55, fig. 3

E1 GOD WITH ROD AND RING (98-9-20) U.3209
Pl. 64
Formerly register III, "obverse"
DESCRIPTION Hard white stone with fine gray grains. A god clasps a ring and rod in his right hand between fingers and thumb, which has the nail indicated. This contrasts with the way objects are held by the seated god on register II, good face. The god wears a robe with clusters of tufts faintly separated by deeper grooves. His beard is divided into five wavy strands, each ending in a single backward spiral.
CONDITION In excellent condition; crisp carving; remnants of a smooth polished film over relief; all old breaks; back dissolved. No salts or bitumen.
FINDSPOT "E.S.B." = "Dub-lal-mak, building southeast of main court"; probably room 17, the only place in that building Woolley lists as a findspot of a stela fragment.[6]
DIMENSIONS GPW 0.095; GPH 0.065; GPTh 0.02 m
PUBLICATION *MJ* 18, p. 96, lower left; *UE* VI, p. 96, pls. 41a, 44f

---

[3] See Gudea stela, *BK* nos. 58, 59.

[4] According to Giegengack, referring to **D1**, "it is unlikely that limestone incorporating so much sulfer could have been deposited in the same oxygen-rich depositional environment in which the major slab of limestone that makes up the bulk of the stela was deposited."

[5] The lack of incrustation could be due to the cleaning the fragments received during two restorations.

[6] *UE* VI, p. 75. This complex belongs in the Ur III period, see Chapter 1, p. 8, nn. 51 and 50.

Index

Plates

PLATE 1

1927 restoration, "good" face.
Photo: UPM neg. 8406

PLATE 2

1927 restoration, "poor" face.
Photo: UPM neg. 8407

PLATE 3

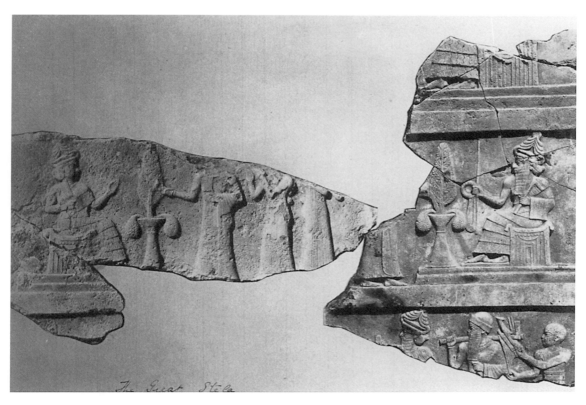

a. 1925 restoration in the field at Ur, registers I–III, "good" face.
   Photo: UPM neg. 46886

b. 1925 restoration at the British Museum, London, registers I–III, "good" face.
   Photo: UPM neg. 8881

PLATE 4

a. Building scene restoration, 1923–24?.
  Photo: UPM neg. 8415

b. Courtyard of the Dublalmakh at Ur, where stela fragments were found, from *UE* VIII, pl. 2a.
  Photo: UPM neg. 8748

PLATE 5

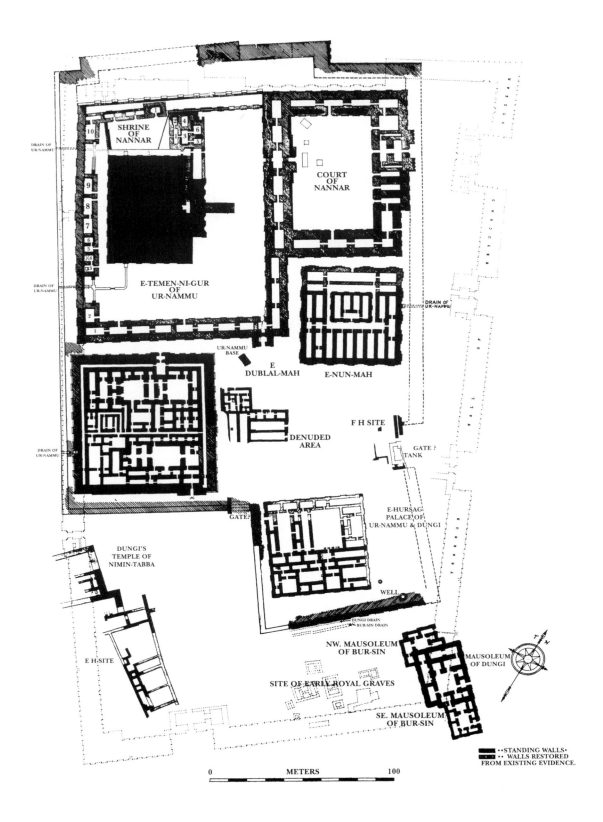

The sacred area of Ur from *UE* VI, pl. 53, with Ur III walls added from plan *UE* VII, pl. 117 and see also *AJ* V, p. 387; and entrance to Ziggurat Terrace corrected by *UE* V, pl. 68 (see Chap. 1, n. 49).

PLATE 6

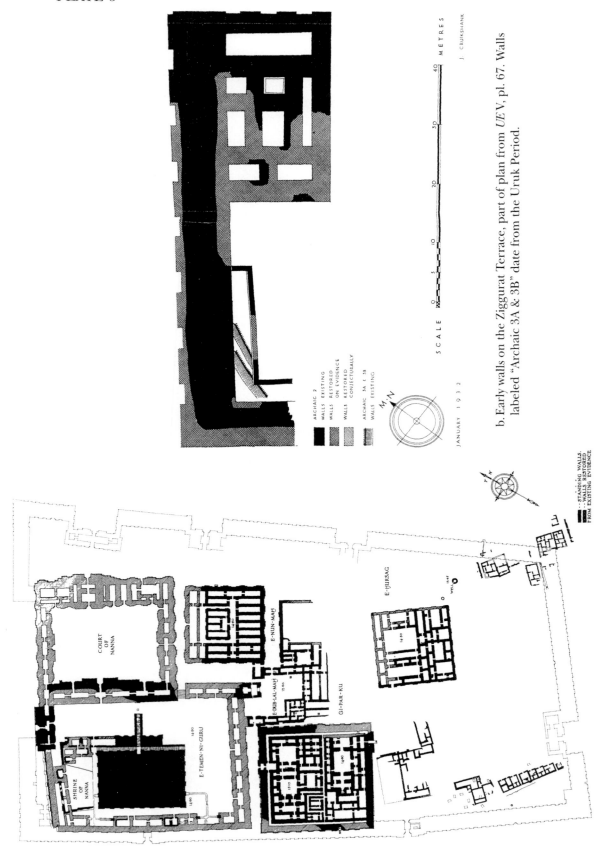

b. Early walls on the Ziggurat Terrace, part of plan from *UE* V, pl. 67. Walls labeled "Archaic 3A & 3B" date from the Uruk Period.

a. The sacred area of Ur in the Larsa Period, from *UE* VII, pl. 117.

PLATE 7

a. **1** poor face, showing stone loss under relief surface.

b. Butchers on **12** poor face, showing chips of relief held together by Woolley's plaster and shellac adhesive.

d. Back of **12** good face, showing large corner fragment with door socket reattached to main block by Woolley.

c. Fragments of **12** poor face, lying in situ on back of **12** good face; note true join of middle fragment.

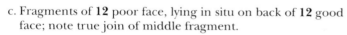

PLATE 8

a. **12** good face, showing area of join to **14** at right, flat cleavage under relief surface, and modern cut to relieve weight.

b. **14**, showing flat natural horizontal cleavage under fragments **a** and **b**, and bitumen dripped onto breaks.

c. Back of **14a** showing ridges and bitumen drips on door socket.

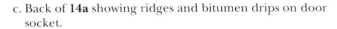

d. Back of **14a–e** with tight joins and with door sockets on **a** (right) and **b** (left).

PLATE 9

a. Top of **28b**, showing bitumen on natural flat break between it and **28a**.

b. **28d** (UET I, no. 44-3, left) and **c** (ibid. 44-2, right) with join under relief surface.

c. Back of basket carrier, **25** (good face), showing modern chiseling to fit it behind drummers, **28a** (poor face).

d. Back of poor face, registers IV and V and inscribed band between, in October 1989, showing techniques of 1927 restoration; wrestlers, **29** (at left), inserted after season of 1932.

PLATE 10

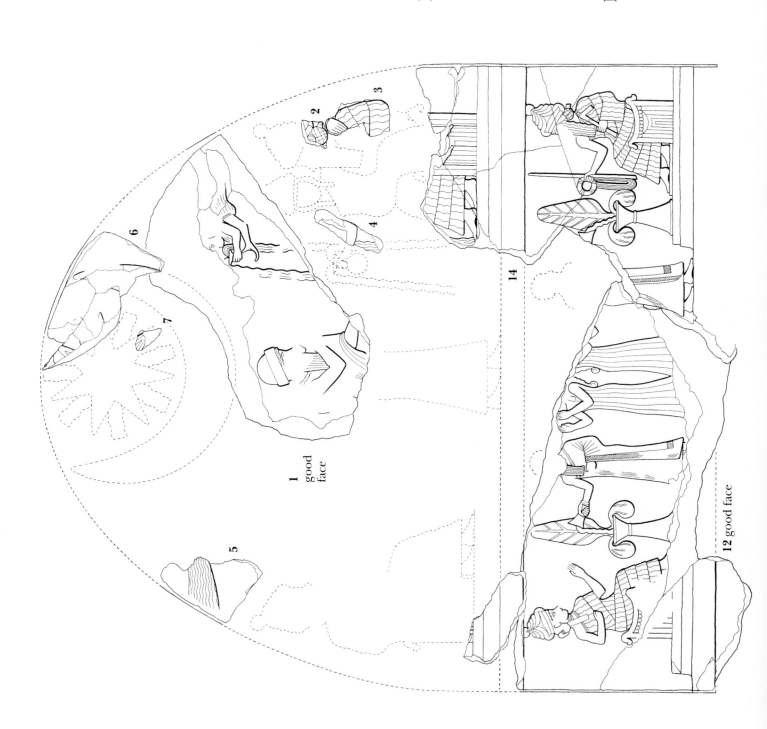

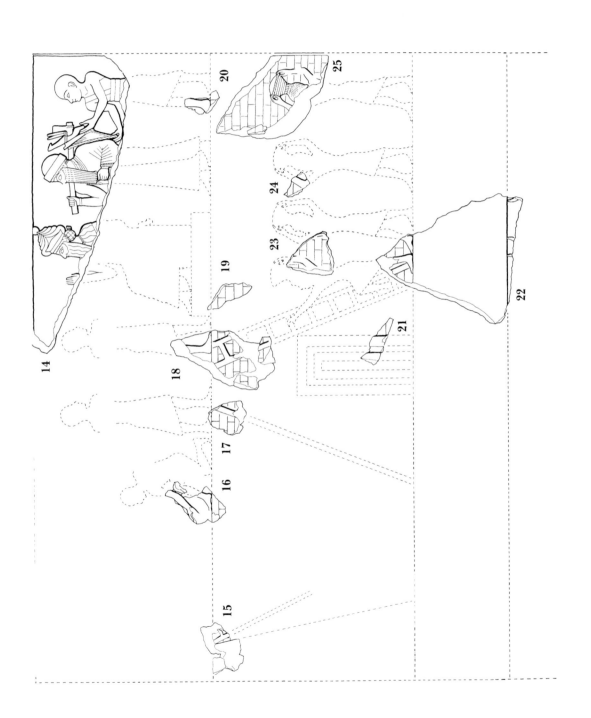

III

IV

V

1:10

New reconstruction, good face.

PLATE 11

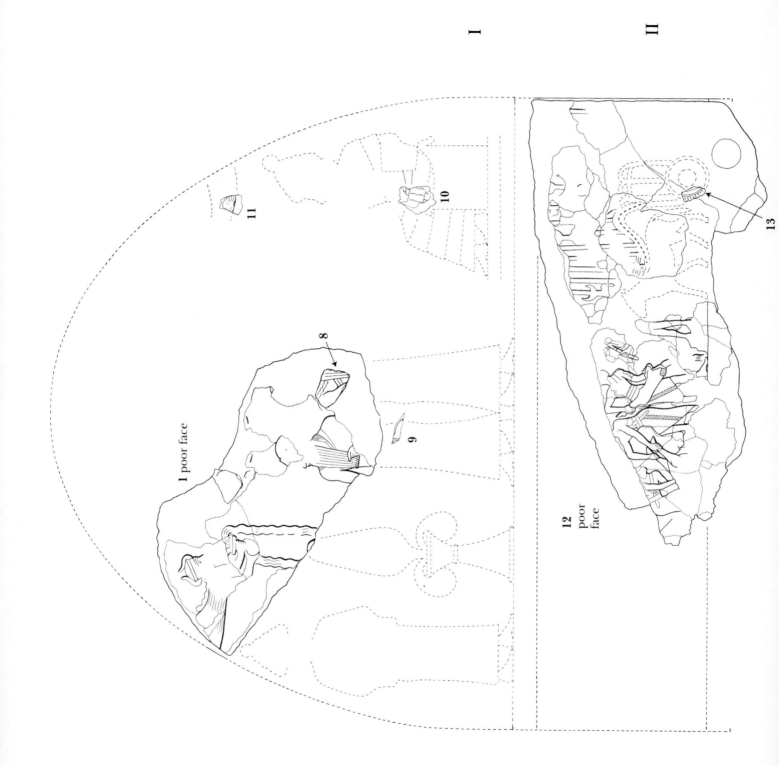

1 poor face

8

9

10

11

12
poor
face

13

I

II

III

IV

V

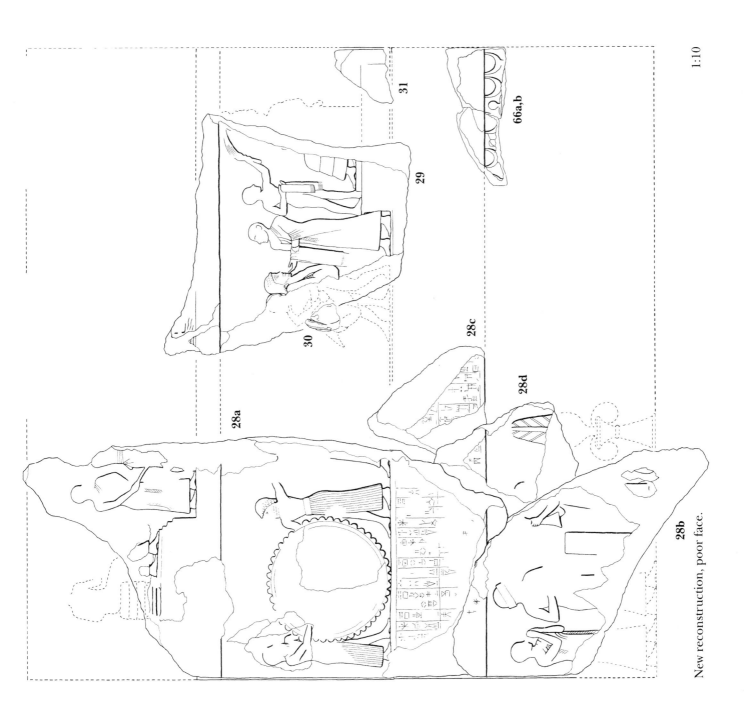

28a

28b

28c

28d

29

30

31

66a,b

New reconstruction, poor face.

1:10

PLATE 12

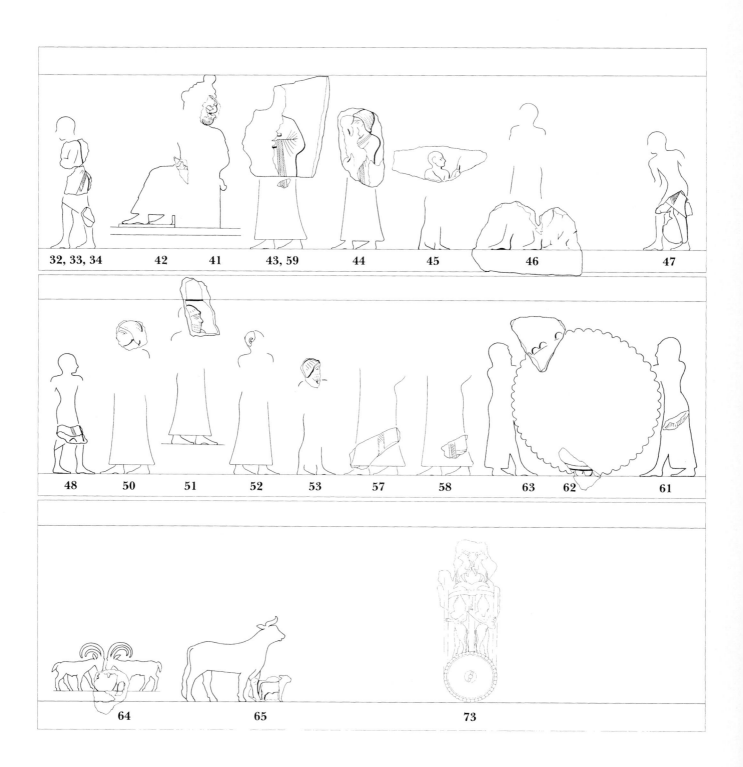

Hypothetical reconstruction of some fragments not placed on the stela.

1:10

PLATE 13

a. God with goddess on
   lap, plaque of Gudea.
   Tello, Iraq, ca. 2000 BC.
   Photo: J. Canby; courtesy
   Museum of the Ancient Near
   East, Istanbul, no. 5552

b. Sealing. Nippur, Iraq, Early Dynastic or Akkadian, late third millennium BC.
   Photo: UPM CBS 11158, neg. S4-143684

PLATE 14

a. Impression of seal of Gudea. Tello,
   Iraq, ca. 2000 BC.
   Drawing: from L. Delaporte, *Catalogue des
   cylindres orienteaux* (Musée du Louvre) I,
   Fouilles et Missions, 108.

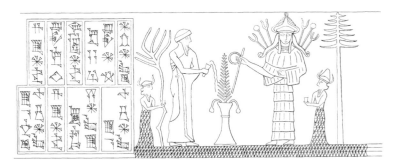

b. Sealing. Nippur, Iraq, ca. 2000 BC (see
   Chap. 3, p. 22, n. 42)
   Drawing: courtesy of R. Zettler

c. Impression on tablet of seal of King Ibbi-Sin of Third
   Dynasty of Ur, seated on tufted stool.
   Photo: UPM CBS 12570

d. Stela. Badra, Iraq, Early Dynastic Period, ca. 2650 BC.
   Drawing: V. Socha after drawing and photographs of F. Safar,
   Sumer 1971, pp. 15–24

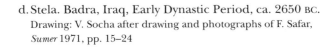

PLATE 15

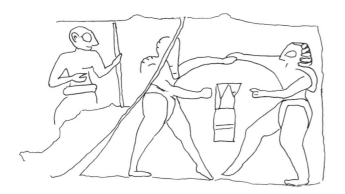

a. Bottom register of plaque. Sin Temple, Khafaje, Iraq, Early Dynastic Period, mid-third millennium BC.
Drawing: after J. Boese, *AfO* 22, 1968/9, fig. 7, p. 35

b. Plaster cast of plaque. Nintu Temple, Khafaje, Iraq, Early Dynastic Period, mid-third millennium BC.
Photo: UPM neg. S4-143685

c. Plaster cast of Nintu Temple plaque.
Drawing: V. Socha

PLATE 16

a. Plaque illustrating a libation to a temple. Ur, Early
Dynastic Period, ca. 2650 BC.
Photo: UPM neg. 9188

b. Foundation deposit of Ur-Nammu.
Nippur, Iraq, ca. 2000 BC.
Photo: courtesy of the Oriental Institute of the
University of Chicago, A30553-55

PLATE 17

1:4

1 good face

PLATE 18

Top of **1** good face, on ground at Ur, already mended
BM photo U.462

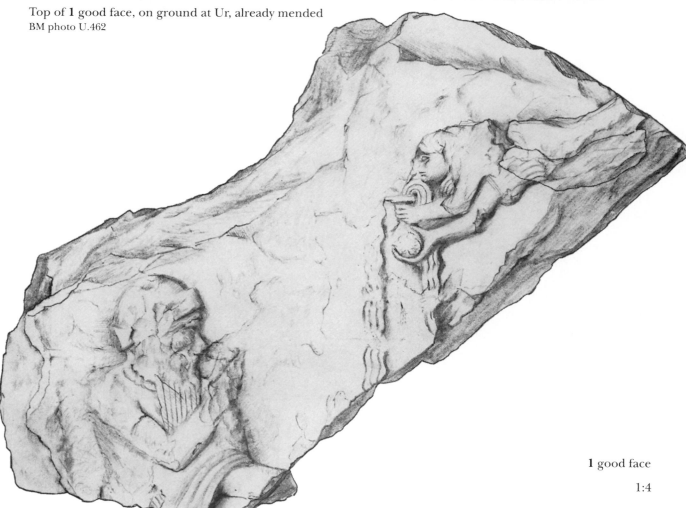

1 good face

1:4

PLATE 19

1:4

1 poor face

PLATE 20

Top of **1** poor face, propped on basket at Ur, already mended
UPM neg. 8879

1 poor face, detail

1:4
detail, no scale

PLATE 21

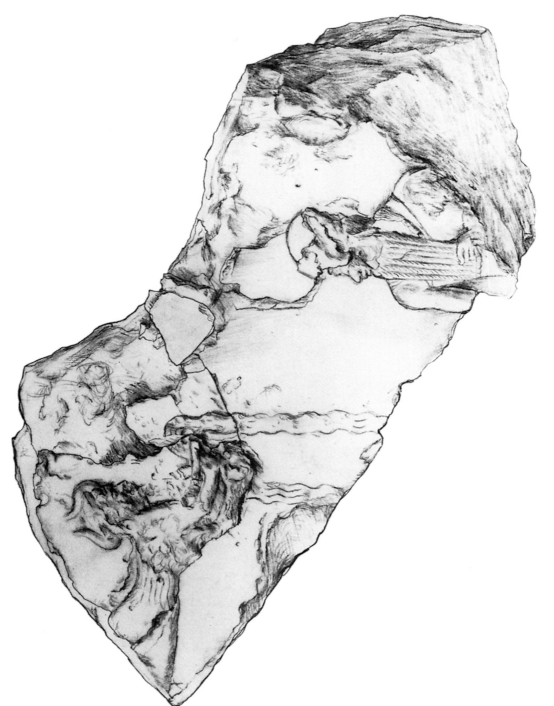

1:4

1 poor face

PLATE 22

2

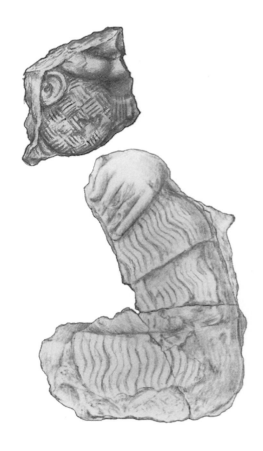

3

4

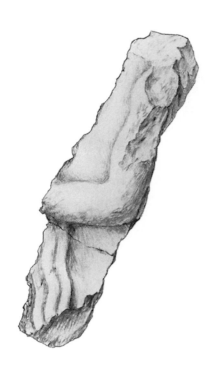

1:2

PLATE 23

5

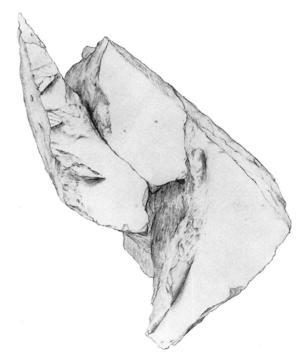

6

1:4

PLATE 24

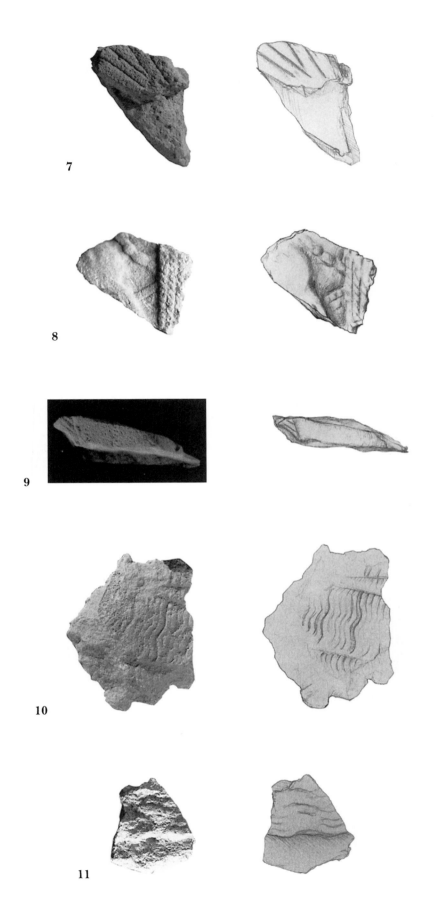

7

8

9

10

11

1:2

PLATE 25

1:5

12 good face

PLATE 26

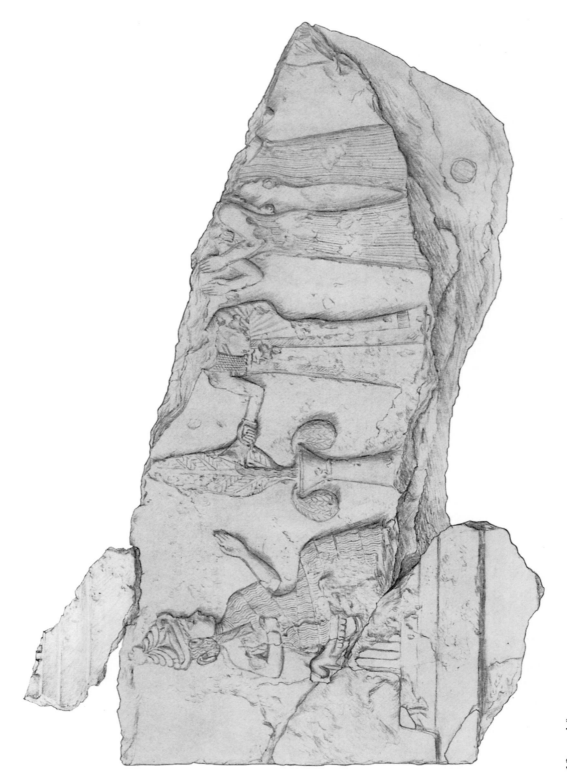

1:5

12 good face

PLATE 27

12 poor face

PLATE 28

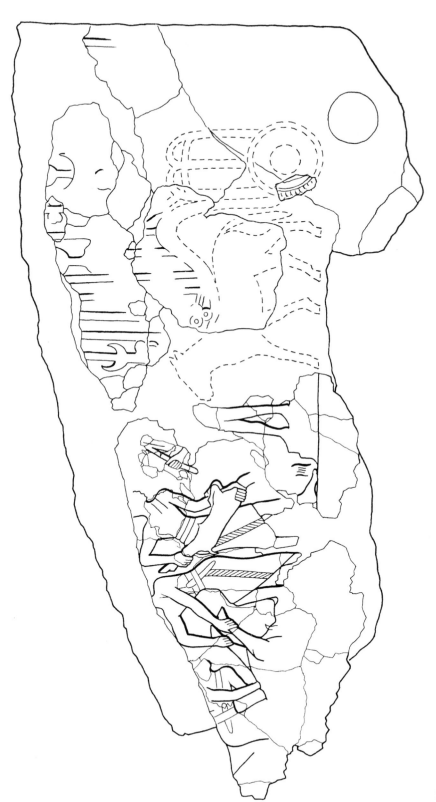

1:5

12 poor face, **13**

PLATE 29

12 poor face, butchering scene, on ground at Ur, already mended
BM photo U.452

12 poor face, butchering scene

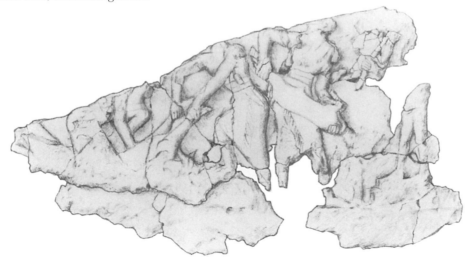

1:5

PLATE 30

12 poor face, standards scene

13

1:5

PLATE 31

14

1:5

PLATE 32

14, detail, original face of god (register II)
UPM neg. S4-140072

14, detail, plaster cast of face of god
(register II) in 1925 restoration

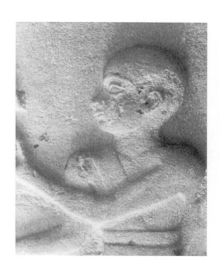

14, details

no scale

PLATE 33

14

1:5

PLATE 34

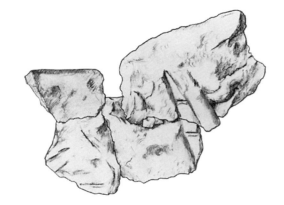

15

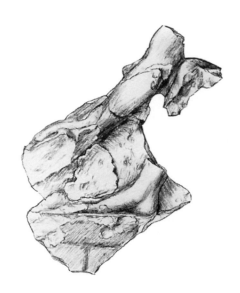

16

17

PLATE 35

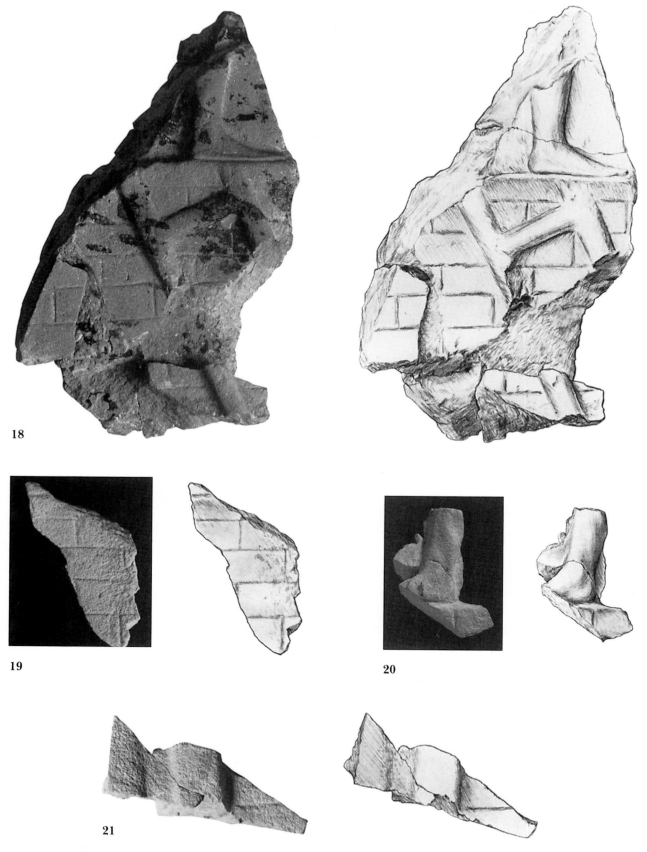

18

19

20

21

1:2

PLATE 36

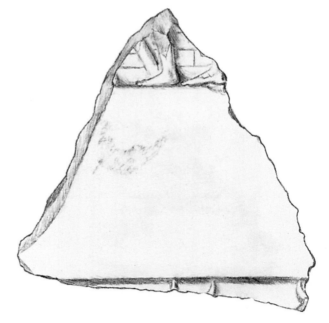

22

23

24

1:2
22, 1:4

PLATE 37

26

27

25

1:2

PLATE 38

PLATE 39

28a, details

no scale

PLATE 40

28a

PLATE 41

28b, detail

28b

1:5
detail, no scale

PLATE 42

28c

 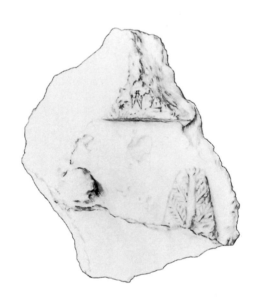

28d

1:5

PLATE 43

29b, detail

29

1:5
detail, no scale

PLATE 44

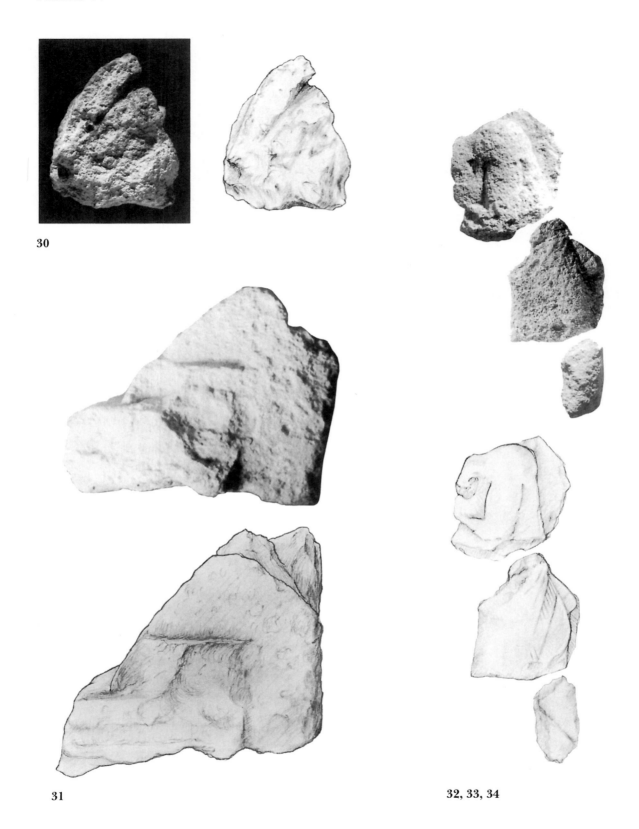

30

31

32, 33, 34

1:2

PLATE 45

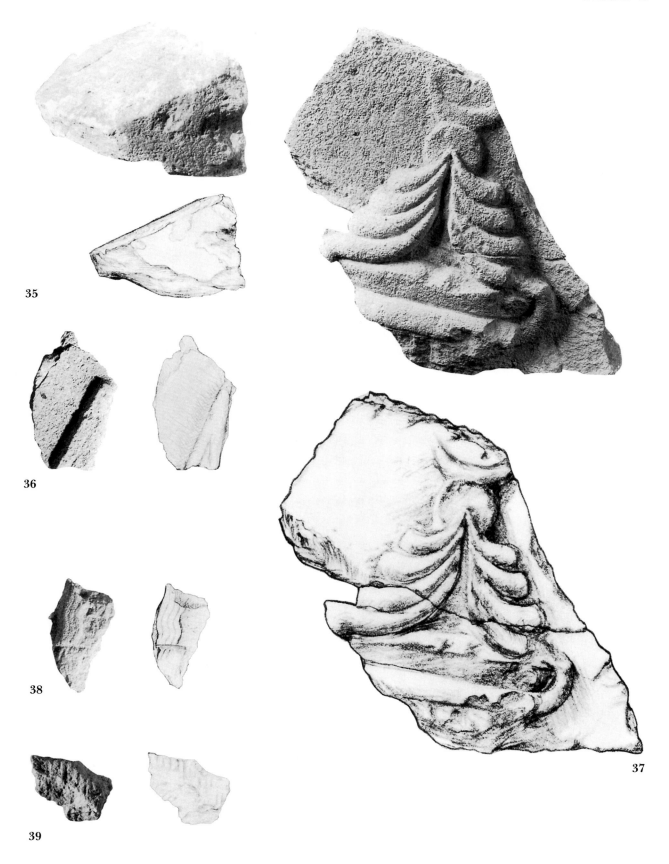

35

36

38

39

37

1:2
35, 1:4

PLATE 46

40

41

42

43

1:2

PLATE 47

44

45

1:2

PLATE 48

46

1:2

PLATE 49

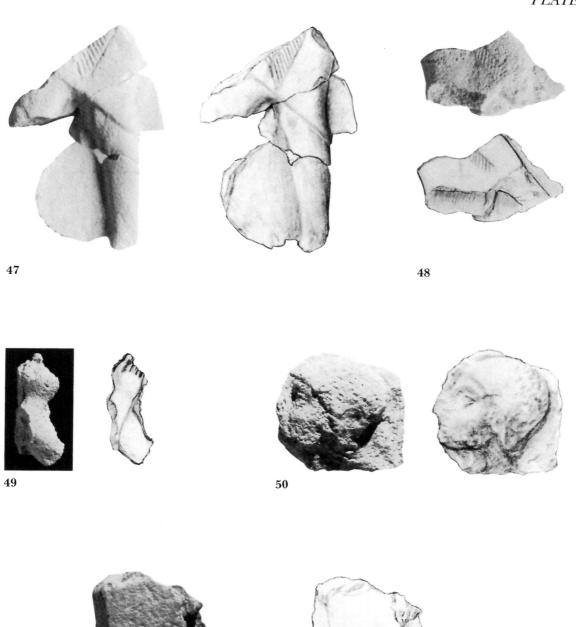

47

48

49

50

51

1:2

PLATE 50

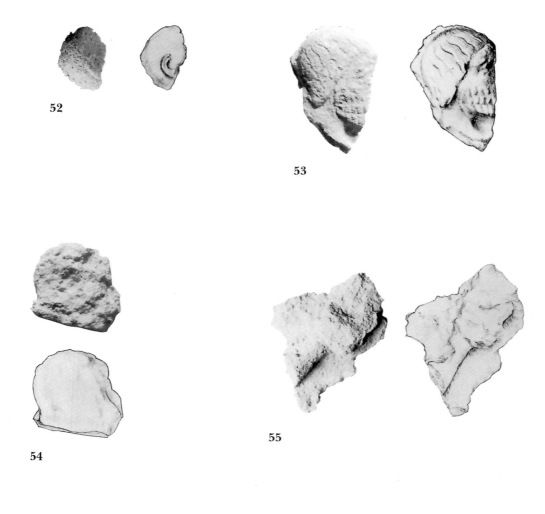

52

53

54

55

56

1:2

PLATE 51

57

58

59

60

61

62

63

1:2

PLATE 52

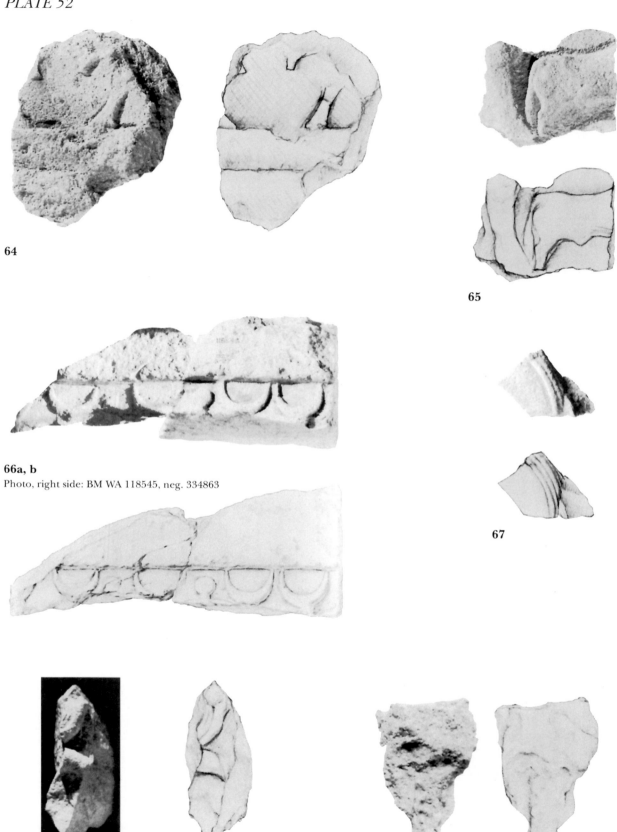

64

65

66a, b
Photo, right side: BM WA 118545, neg. 334863

67

68

69

1:2
66a, b, 1:4

PLATE 53

70

71

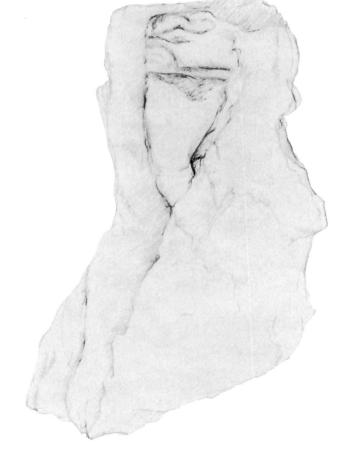

72

1:2

PLATE 54

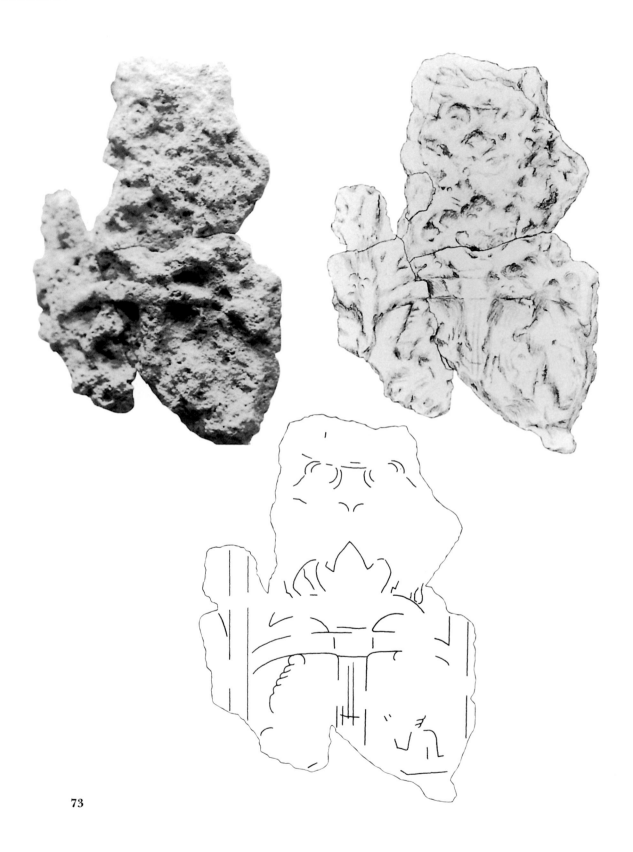

73

1:2

PLATE 55

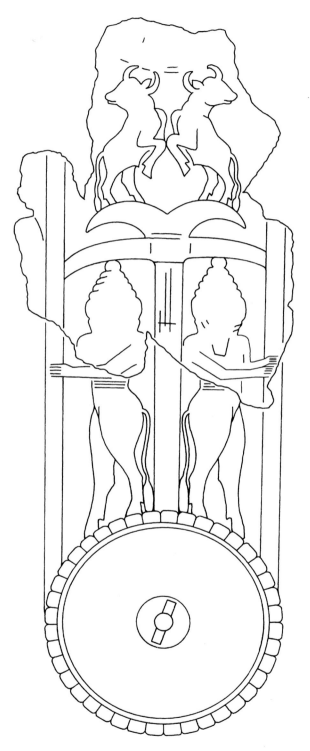

73

1:2

PLATE 56

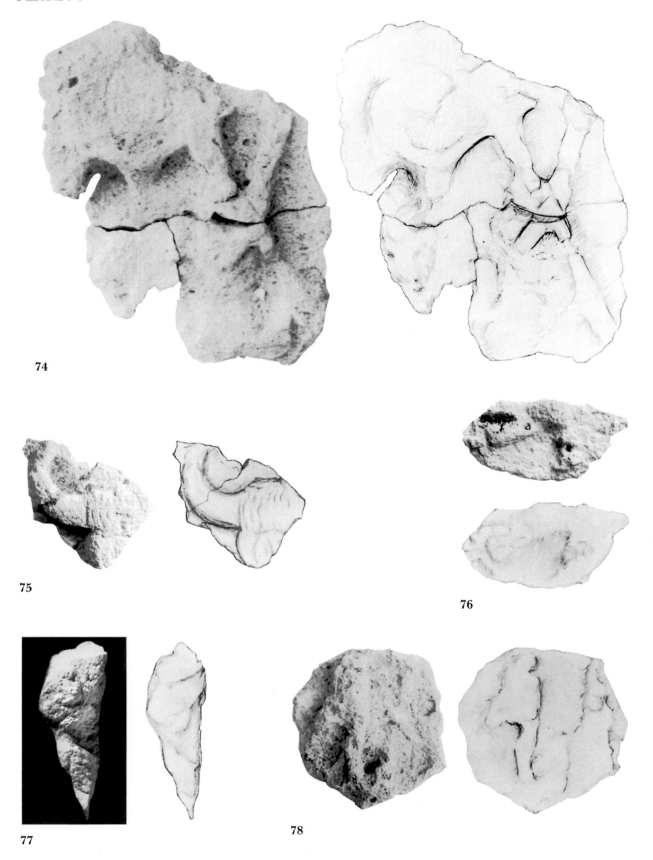

74

75

76

77

78

1:2

PLATE 57

79

81

80

82

83

84

1:2
84, 1:4

PLATE 58

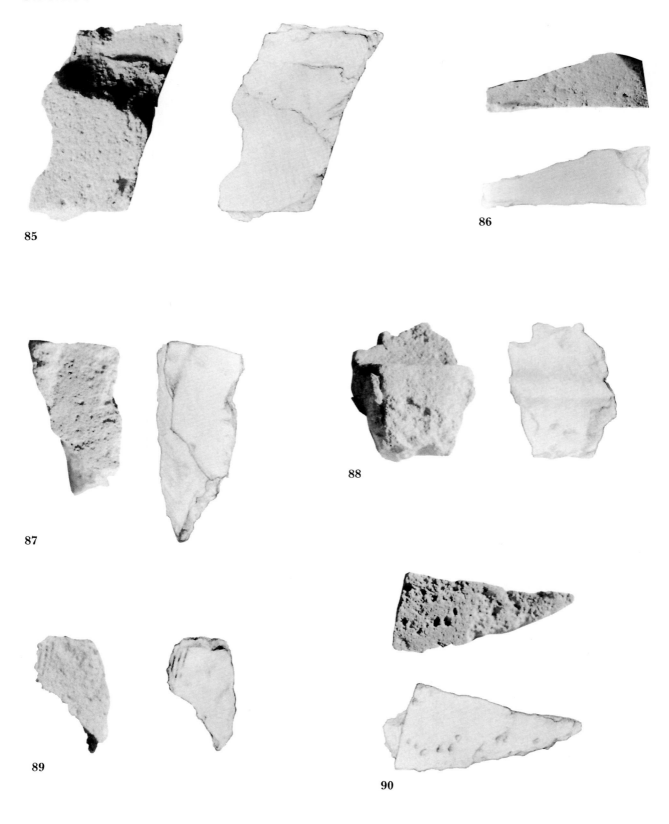

85

86

87

88

89

90

1:2
86, 1:4

PLATE 59

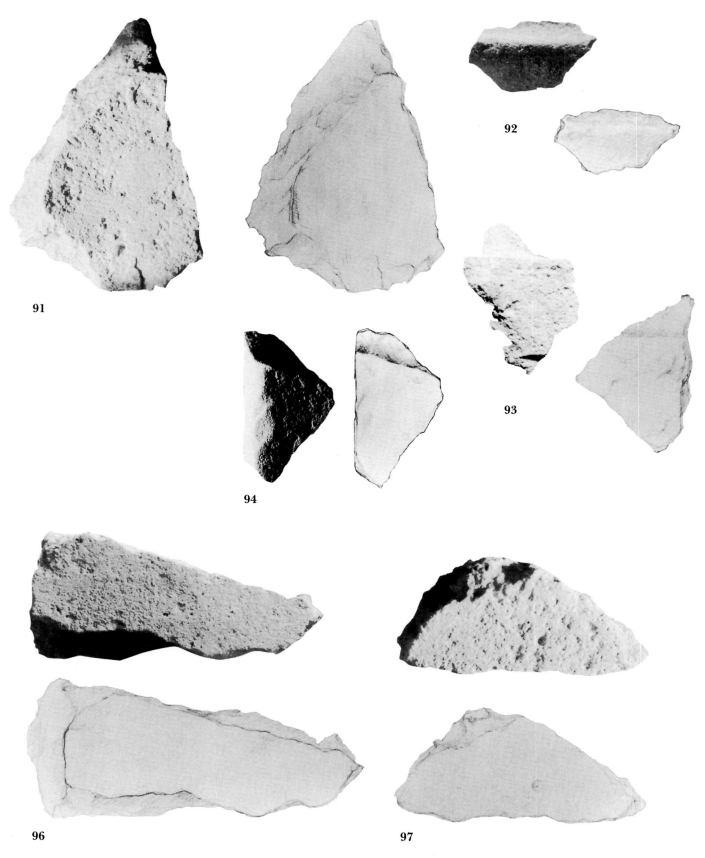

91

92

93

94

96

97

1:2

PLATE 60

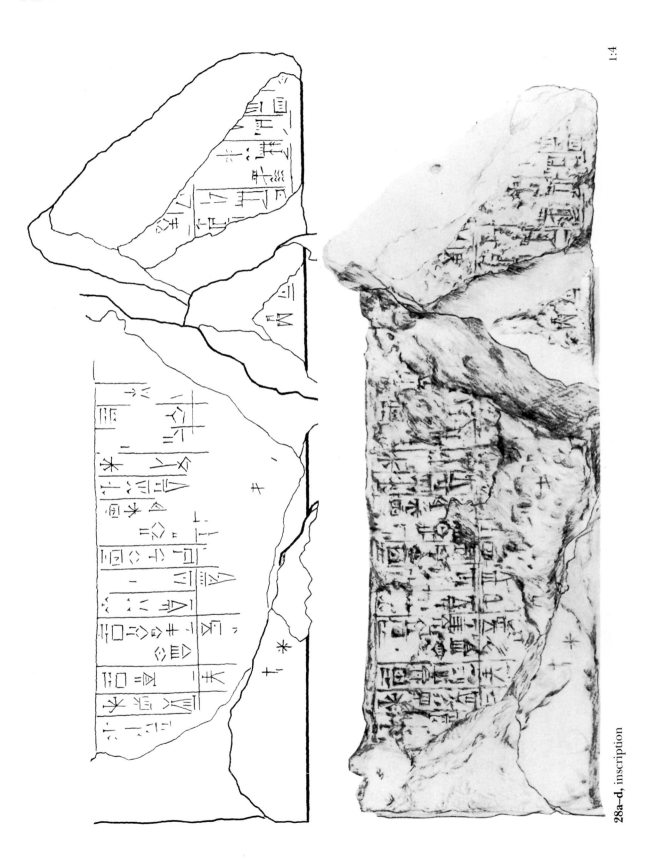

1:4

28a–d, inscription

PLATE 61

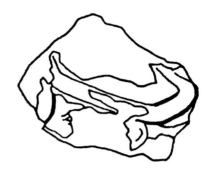

A1

A2

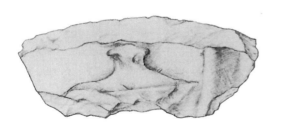
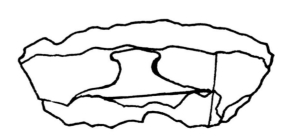

B1

1:2

PLATE 62

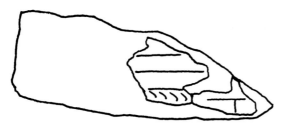

B2

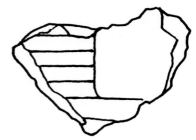

B3

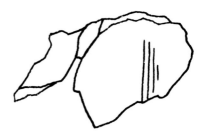

C1

C2

1:2

PLATE 63

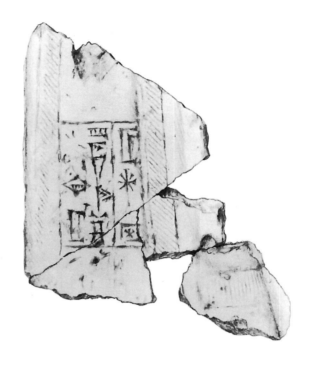

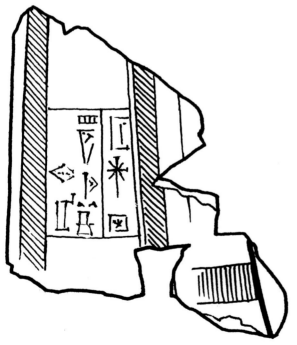

D1

D1 in 1927 restoration, absent right
fringe fragment

1:2
detail, no scale

PLATE 64

  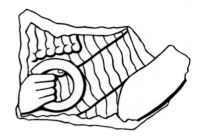

E1

1:2